Beauty and Catechesis

Beauty and Catechesis

Gaven M. Mize

Foreword by John Pless

Kasandra M. Radke, publisher

© 2017 Gaven M. Mize, author, all rights reserved.

© 2017 Ryan W. Porter, cover layout, all rights reserved.

Edited by Sarah Ludwig Rausch
Layout by Patricia Ludwig
Special thanks to Katie Hill and Joshua Mize

All images are in the public domain, taken from Wikimedia Commons.

The Litany by Johann Konrad Wilhelm Löhe is in the public domain.

Ending collect prayers are from Rev. Bryan Wolfmueller, Rev. Steven Anderson,
and Rev. Gaven Mize.

Luther's Small Catechism (Triglotta) is in the public domain.
http://bookofconcord.org/smallcatechism.php

ISBN: 978-0-9835488-6-7   Softcover edition/ July 2017

Printed in the United States of America
1357908642

Grail Quest Books can be found at http://www.grailquestbooks.com
Other works of Rev. Mize can be found at http://www.mizefamilybooks.com

*To my brother, Joshua Mize, who above all reason
stood by me in all my triumphs and troubles.*

*To Tuesday, my brother's wonderful wife, and
their beautiful daughters, Harper and Quinn.*

*To the members of Augustana Evangelical Lutheran
Church in Hickory, North Carolina, in full appreciation
for your love for Christ, the faith, the Confessions,
and for caring for your pastor.*

*This work is for your family, that you would continue
to be edified in the word of our dear Lord.*

Contents

Foreword

Beauty and Catechesis combines a judicious use of classical art, succinct meditations, and short prayers, once again demonstrating how Luther's Small Catechism is a multi-faceted book of doctrine, prayer, and life. Too often, the Catechism is considered only as an easily mastered elementary and basic introduction to Christian doctrine, only to be set aside for books and manuals that allegedly go deeper into the Bible and hold out a more contemporary approach to Christian life. Pastor Gaven Mize demonstrates the contrary. The Catechism in its simplicity embraces not only the depth of the Christian faith, but also its beauty.

It is no wonder, then, that the Formula of Concord would come to call the Catechism "a Bible of the Laity, in which everything is summarized that is treated in detail in Holy Scripture and that is necessary for a Christian to know for salvation" (FC Ep I, 5, Kolb-Wengert, 487). Commandments, Creed, and the Lord's Prayer, drawn from the Scriptures, form the core of the Catechism. Luther adds Baptism and the Lord's Supper, anchoring both in the words of Jesus that institute them, unpacks their benefits, and tutors us in how faith receives the gifts. In time, Luther would also insert a short form of confession between Baptism and the Sacrament of the Altar. Our duty "to thank, praise, serve and obey" (First Article) is given concrete form in the daily prayers and the Table of Duties appended to the Catechism. God's Law (Ten Commandments) brings us to see our sin. The gospel of the triune God is embodied in the Apostles' Creed. Faith calls on the Father in the words His Son has given us to pray (The Lord's Prayer). Faith receives the gifts Jesus designates in baptism, in the words of absolution, and with His body and blood in the Supper. Lives made holy by the Spirit are lived in the "holy orders" of congregation, community, and home. The Catechism is geared toward repentance, faith, and holy living. Listen for this recurring theme in the meditations you are about to read and ponder.

Learning the Christian faith is not an academic exercise for Luther but rather it is a life that is lived in the promises of God and under the cross that puts to death the old man driving us back to Christ alone. God is not the object of our study but the One who is acting in us through His word. He does the verbs of salvation. Creation, redemption, and sanctification are

His works. We are on the receiving end without "any merit or worthiness of mine" (SC II, 2, Kolb-Wengert, 354). Praying the Catechism locates us in the pattern of His giving, our receiving His gifts, and the fruition of His gifts on our lips and in our lives.

Paul exhorted Timothy to *"Follow the pattern of the sound words that you have heard from me in the faith and love that are in Christ Jesus"* (2 Timothy 1:13). This is what we are given in the Catechism, "the pattern of the sound words . . . in the faith and love that are in Christ Jesus." This pattern guides us in our confession, that is, the speaking of the true words about God received from Him. Faith confesses Christ. Love hands on to our neighbor the gifts that we have been given. We remain students. Listen to Luther:

> I am also a doctor and a preacher, just as learned and experienced as all of them who are so high and mighty. Nevertheless, each morning and whenever else I have time, I do as a child who is being taught the catechism and I read and recite word for word the Lord's Prayer, the Ten Commandments, the Creed, the Psalms etc. I must still read and study the catechism—and I also do so gladly. (Preface to the Large Catechism, Kolb-Wengert, 380)

This little book by Pastor Gaven M. Mize invites you to meditate on the riches stored in the Small Catechism. It is a meditation that involves the mind, heart, and eye as readers are drawn into the simple beauty embedded in Luther's confession of the biblical faith. This book, like the Catechism itself, is not for a quick, one-time reading, but promises to be an ongoing companion for spiritual refreshment and edification.

~ Prof. John T. Pless
Concordia Theological Seminary
Fort Wayne, Indiana
Monday in Lent IV, 2017

Introduction

"Beauty is the disinterested one, without which the ancient world refused to understand itself, a word which both imperceptibly and yet unmistakably has bid farewell to our new world, a world of interests, leaving it to its own avarice and sadness."

~ *Hans Urs von Balthasar*
Twentieth-century theologian of aesthetics

Too many have believed for far too long that Martin Luther's Small Catechism is a nice addition to catechesis, but that there are better options available for the building of faith. To this I would say that those who believe this have not seen the scriptural beauty that is so deeply ingrained in the Six Chief Parts of the catechism. The Small Catechism was written by Martin Luther for those in the real world with real world problems, who did not have a place to find God's law and gospel. Today, we have English translations of the Bible, which the large majority of Christians can read. However, the Scriptures can seem like a jigsaw puzzle both in times of peril and in times of edification through scriptural meditation. Luther's Small Catechism, as well as the entire Book of Concord, is the box top to the jigsaw puzzle that guides us in putting the pieces of law and gospel together into a beautiful work of art that one can take in again and again in times of need.

There never was the promise that life would be easy. No one ever promised happiness. God's presence was the promise: in the supper; in the waters. We may bemoan that God has allowed things in our lives that rattle us, and we may try to hold Him to promises of glee and bliss on this earth that were never made. In the end, there is only the incarnation and the resurrection, and in between those, there is only the crucifixion. So, when our time of dying comes and we look around for the promises of God, we will find the death of Jesus, and, in that death, we will find life in God. These teachings are unfolded in Luther's Small Catechism. The Six Chief Parts point us to the biblical truths in such a way that everyone can understand them. To teach our children and catechumens these chief parts is the height of familial responsibility.

When we are pressed to give an account for the truth that is within us or when we have been brought low by tragedy or death, what words will we remember? When we seem to be straying from the truth, what tastes shall we taste that are the goodness of God? When we can't seem to get out of our minds the image of the last moments of a loved one dying, what image shall we concentrate on that reassures us of the faith that was given to them and us? What smells bring us back to prayer? What senses drag us back to God, both kicking and screaming, as well as willingly? The salutary tools we use to stimulate our senses must be centered in Scripture as an aid for our edification and retention.

For this reason, I have compiled this version of Martin Luther's Small Catechism. The art that is coupled with the beautiful words of Martin Luther is meant to engage both hearing and sight, which allow and encourage not only retention, but also connect each chief part with biblical and historical truths. Please keep in mind that not all the pieces of art that I have chosen to pair with each section are from biblical narratives. However, the ones I chose are renditions of some of the most well-known stories throughout the world.

I chose each piece for two main purposes: (1) So that the reader would be able to retain Luther's Small Catechism more easily and (2) that the reader would come to appreciate beauty in Christ's catholic church. May we grow in appreciation of catechetical aesthetics so the next generation of Lutherans will grow more firmly in the evangelical faith and liturgical practice.

There will come a day when every member of the next generation will face life-altering decisions, sickness, decline of the faithful, potential punishment for the faith, and eventually death. What will they say about the faith at these times? When all else fails, including our hearts, there is always Christ crucified and the merits from it that flow to cup and font. The truth of these merits is laid out in the beautiful words of Martin Luther. May we find the constant beauty in the Small Catechism and hold firm to it, and suffer, even to death, rather than fall away from those truths that point us back to the foundations of Christ's own Scripture.

In this simple work, it is my hope that readers will come to piece together the words of Luther, the historic works of art, and the narratives to help them grow in knowledge with ease and enjoyment. For you, dear reader, I am grateful. May you be richly blessed in your reading. But, more importantly, flee to the pew, the font, and the altar of our God. After all, we must be fed as the rubber of theology hits the road of our transgressions. There, as Luther points out, is forgiveness of sins, life, and salvation.

Beauty and Catechesis

MARTIN LUTHER'S
SMALL CATECHISM

Woodcut by Hans Brosamer of the Last Supper from the 1550 AD
Frankfurt Edition of the Small Catechism of Martin Luther

British School's *Martin Luther* (Before 1626 AD)

Luther's Preface to the Small Catechism

Martin Luther to All Faithful and Godly Pastors and Preachers:

Grace, Mercy, and Peace in Jesus Christ, our Lord.

The deplorable, miserable condition which I discovered lately when I, too, was a visitor, has forced and urged me to prepare [publish] this Catechism, or Christian doctrine, in this small, plain, simple form. Mercy! Good God! what manifold misery I beheld! The common people, especially in the villages, have no knowledge whatever of Christian doctrine, and, alas! many pastors are altogether incapable and incompetent to teach [so much so, that one is ashamed to speak of it]. Nevertheless, all maintain that they are Christians, have been baptized and receive the [common] holy Sacraments. Yet they [do not understand and] cannot [even] recite either the Lord's Prayer, or the Creed, or the Ten Commandments; they live like dumb brutes and irrational hogs; and yet, now that the Gospel has come, they have nicely learned to abuse all liberty like experts.

O ye bishops! [to whom this charge has been committed by God,] what will ye ever answer to Christ for having so shamefully neglected the people and never for a moment discharged your office? [You are the persons to whom alone this ruin of the Christian religion is due. You have permitted men to err so shamefully; yours is the guilt; for you have ever done anything rather than what your office required you to do.] May all misfortune flee you! [I do not wish at this place to invoke evil on your heads.] You command the Sacrament in one form [but is not this the highest ungodliness coupled with the greatest impudence that you are insisting on the administration of the Sacrament in one form only, and on your traditions] and insist on your human laws, and yet at the same time you do not care in the least [while you are utterly without scruple and concern] whether the people know the Lord's Prayer, the Creed, the Ten Commandments, or any part of the Word of God. Woe, woe, unto you forever!

Therefore I entreat [and adjure] you all for God's sake, my dear sirs and brethren, who are pastors or preachers, to devote yourselves heartily to your office, to have pity on the people who are entrusted to you, and to help us inculcate the Catechism upon the people, and especially upon the young. And let those of you who cannot do better [If any of you are so unskilled that you have absolutely no knowledge of these matters, let them not be ashamed to] take these tables and forms and impress them, word for word, on the people, as follows:

In the first place, let the preacher above all be careful to avoid many kinds of or various texts and forms of the Ten Commandments, the Lord's Prayer, the Creed, the Sacraments, etc., but choose one form to which he adheres, and which he inculcates all the time, year after year. For [I give this advice, however, because I know that] young and simple people must be taught by uniform, settled texts and forms, otherwise they easily become confused when the teacher to-day teaches them thus, and in a year some other way, as if he wished to make improvements, and thus all effort and labor [which has been expended in teaching] is lost.

Also our blessed fathers understood this well; for they all used the same form of the Lord's Prayer, the Creed, and the Ten Commandments. Therefore we, too, should [imitate their diligence and be at pains to] teach the young and simple people these parts in such a way as not to change a syllable, or set them forth and repeat them one year differently than in another [no matter how often we teach the Catechism].

Hence, choose whatever form you please, and adhere to it forever. But when you preach in the presence of learned and intelligent men, you may exhibit your skill, and may present these parts in as varied and intricate ways and give them as masterly turns as you are able. But with the young people stick to one fixed, permanent form and manner, and teach them, first of all, these parts, namely, the Ten Commandments, the Creed, the Lord's Prayer, etc., according to the text, word for word, so that they, too, can repeat it in the same manner after you and commit it to memory.

But those who are unwilling to learn it should be told that they deny Christ and are no Christians, neither should they be admitted to the Sacrament, accepted as sponsors at baptism, nor exercise any part of Christian liberty, but should simply be turned back to the Pope and his officials, yea, to the devil himself. Moreover, their parents and employers should refuse them food and drink, and [they would also do well if they were to] notify them that the prince will drive such rude people from the country, etc.

For although we cannot and should not force any one to believe, yet we should insist and urge the people that they know what is right and wrong with those among whom they dwell and wish to make their living. For whoever desires to reside in a town must know and observe the town laws, the protection of which he wishes to enjoy, no matter whether he is a believer or at heart and in private a rogue or knave.

In the second place, after they have well learned the text, then teach them the sense also, so that they know what it means, and again choose the form of these tables, or some other brief uniform method, whichever you like, and adhere to it, and do not change a single syllable, as was just said regarding the text; and take your time to it. For it is not necessary that you take up all the parts at once, but one after the other. After they understand the First Commandment well, then take up the Second, and so on, otherwise they will be overwhelmed, so as not to be able to retain any well.

In the third place, after you have thus taught them this Short Catechism, then take up the Large Catechism, and give them also a richer and fuller knowledge. Here explain at large every commandment, [article,] petition, and part with its various works, uses, benefits, dangers, and injuries, as you find these abundantly stated in many books written about these matters. And particularly, urge that commandment or part most which suffers the greatest neglect among your people. For instance, the Seventh Commandment, concerning stealing, must be strenuously urged among mechanics and merchants, and even farmers and servants, for among these people many kinds of dishonesty and thieving prevail. So, too, you must urge well the Fourth Commandment among the children and the common people, that they may be quiet and faithful, obedient and peaceable, and you must always adduce many examples from the Scriptures to show how God has punished or blessed such persons.

Especially should you here urge magistrates and parents to rule well and to send their children to school, showing them why it is their duty to do this, and what a damnable sin they are committing if they do not do it. For by such neglect they overthrow and destroy both the kingdom of God and that of the world, acting as the worst enemies both of God and of men. And make it very plain to them what an awful harm they are doing if they will not help to train children to be pastors, preachers, clerks [also for other offices, with which we cannot dispense in this life], etc., and that God will punish them terribly for it. For such preaching is needed. [Verily, I do not know of any other topic that deserves to be treated as much as this.] Parents and magistrates are now sinning unspeakably in this respect. The devil, too, aims at something cruel because of these things [that he may hurl Germany into the greatest distress].

Lastly, since the tyranny of the Pope has been abolished, people are no longer willing to go to the Sacrament and despise it [as something useless and unnecessary]. Here again urging is necessary, however, with this understanding: We are to force no one to believe, or to receive the Sacrament, nor fix any law, nor time, nor place for it, but are to preach in such a manner that of their own accord, without our law, they will urge themselves and, as it were, compel us pastors to administer the Sacrament. This is done by telling them: Whoever does not seek or desire the Sacrament at least some four times a year, it is to be feared that he despises the Sacrament and is no Christian, just as he is no Christian who does not believe or hear the Gospel; for Christ did not say, This omit, or, This despise, but, *This do ye, as oft as ye drink it*, etc. Verily, He wants it done, and not entirely neglected and despised. *This do* ye, He says.

Now, whoever does not highly value the Sacrament thereby shows that he has no sin, no flesh, no devil, no world, no death, no danger, no hell; that is, he does not believe any such things, although he is in them over head and ears and is doubly the devil's own. On the other hand, he needs no grace, life, Paradise, heaven, Christ, God, nor anything good. For if he believed that he had so much that is evil, and needed so much that is good, he would not thus neglect the Sacrament, by which such evil is remedied and so much good is bestowed. Neither will it be necessary to force him to the Sacrament by any law, but he will come running and racing of his own accord, will force himself and urge you that you must give him the Sacrament.

Hence, you must not make any law in this matter, as the Pope does. Only set forth clearly the benefit and harm, the need and use, the danger and the blessing, connected with this Sacrament, and the people will come of themselves without your compulsion. But if they do not come, let them go and tell them that such belong to the devil as do not regard nor feel their great need and the gracious help of God. But if you do not urge this, or make a law or a bane of it, it is your fault if they despise the Sacrament. How could they be otherwise than slothful if you sleep and are silent? Therefore look to it, ye pastors and preachers. Our office is now become a different thing from what it was under the Pope; it is now become serious and salutary. Accordingly, it now involves much more trouble and labor, danger and trials, and, in addition thereto, little reward and gratitude in the world. But Christ Himself will be our reward if we labor faithfully. To this end may the Father of all grace help us, to whom be praise and thanks forever through Christ, our Lord! Amen.

THE TEN COMMANDMENTS

Philippe de Champaigne's *Moses with the Ten Commandments* (1648 AD)

The First Commandment

Thou shalt have no other gods.

What does this mean?

We should fear, love, and trust in God above all things.

Rembrandt's *Daniel and Cyrus Before the Idol Bel* (1633 AD)

This painting by Rembrandt shines a new light (quite literally with his choice of bright colors surrounding Daniel) on the Apocryphal books. Martin Luther himself once commented that the Apocrypha, while not meant to be held to the level of canonical Scriptures, is very useful and edifying for the theologian and reader to absorb. That is seemingly quite true, as before us we find an excellent example of both keeping and breaking the First Commandment.

In the fourteenth chapter of the Apocryphal additions to the book of Daniel, after King Astyages died, his successor, Cyrus of Persia, was with Daniel, who was treated with love and honor by all around. The king was a worshiper of the idol Bel, and noticed that Daniel would not worship Bel as he did. He asked Daniel why he didn't believe that Bel was a god of flesh and blood, since Cyrus had seen proof of all that Bel had eaten and drunk. Daniel, who would not be swayed from the faith, answered that Bel was an idol made of clay and covered with mere bronze. The king challenged Daniel to test whether Bel was alive and ate food or if he was indeed merely an idol. The priests of Bel were to lay flour, sheep, and much wine in front of Bel and seal the temple with all inside. If Bel did not consume all in front of him, then the priests were to be killed, but if he did, then Daniel was to be killed.

Daniel was a wise man. He scattered ashes over the floor of the temple to catch the priests who had been creeping in and consuming the food for themselves and then pretending that it was the false idol Bel who had eaten it. When the sun rose the next morning, Daniel showed King Cyrus the footprints in the ash that the priests had made. The priests confessed and showed all where the secret passageway was that they had been using to fool everyone. For their lies and treachery, the priests and their families were put to death. Then Daniel was permitted to do the very thing all Christians are called to do: Daniel destroyed the temple and the idol of Bel and worshiped the one true Triune God.

In the name of the Father, and of the ✝ Son, and of the Holy Spirit.

O Majestic Trinity, You have given unto us grace beyond measure. Grant us the wisdom and faith to profess the one true God, and by that profession of the true faith, acknowledge the glory of the eternal Trinity, and, in the power of Your divine majesty, to worship the unity; through Christ our Lord, who lives and reigns with the Father and the Holy Spirit, now and forever. *Amen.*

The Second Commandment

Thou shalt not take the name of the Lord, thy God, in vain.

What does this mean?

We should fear and love God that we may not curse, swear, use witchcraft, lie, or deceive by His name, but call upon it in every trouble, pray, praise, and give thanks.

Temptation of Christ **Mosaic in Basilica di San Marco**
(Twelfth century AD)

In Venice, Italy, stands the Basilica di San Marco, which is known for its beautiful liturgical architecture, history, amazing works of art, and most famously, its mosaic pieces. Mosaic is a unique and eye-catching form of art created by strategically and carefully placing hundreds of tiny (and in some cases, not so tiny) pieces of stone. Each stone has a purpose and is essential in proclaiming grand images from Scripture. In this way mosaics are much like the bride of Christ, which is His church. The art is formed by each rock, placed with great care and love, not unlike the gospel truth of our Lord Jesus Christ, who was begotten by God the Father, the artist of all creation.

In this mosaic created by an unknown artist, the little stones are brought together to teach us of Christ's temptations by Satan. In the biblical account, if Satan could get Christ to sinfully act on the temptations, then Christ could not have fulfilled the law for us. Satan's angle of attack against Christ was to twist the word and name of God the Father, much like he did to Eve in the Garden of Eden.

The first temptation from Satan was to try to take advantage of Christ being hungry after not eating for forty days. Satan blasphemed against Christ by one simple word: "if," saying that if Christ was the Son of God, then He would be able to turn stones into bread. Christ responded to Satan by simply quoting Scripture. Satan then changed the angle of attack by taking Christ to the highest point of the temple and blasphemed against Him by distorting God's word, yet Christ responded once again by speaking the word of God. Finally, Satan took Christ to a high mountain and promised Christ all that they could see. Christ once again spoke the same word of God Satan hears concerning us at the baptismal font: *"Away from me."*

While Satan misused the name of God and twisted the word of God, Christ remained without sin during His temptation. By this and the all-availing sacrifice, Christ remained and remains our champion and victor over sin, death, and the devil. May we also in times of temptation not curse God's name, but call upon His name in prayer, praise, and thanksgiving.

In the name of the Father, and of the ✛ Son, and of the Holy Spirit.

Almighty and most merciful God, You graciously hear our prayers. Free our hearts from the temptations of evil thoughts, that we may flee to Your most holy name and not despise it, swear against it, or blaspheme it for the sake of our souls; in the name of Your Son, Jesus Christ, who lives and reigns with You and the Holy Spirit, now and forever. *Amen.*

The Third Commandment

Thou shalt sanctify the holy-day.

What does this mean?

We should fear and love God that we may not despise preaching and His Word, but hold it sacred, and gladly hear and learn it.

Julius Schnorr von Carolsfeld's Woodcut of *The Sabbath* from *Die Bibel in Bildern* (1851–1860 AD)

Woodcutting was a way of getting art into the hands of the people through mass production. The earliest known Christian woodcut was found around 1400 AD in Italy. It was Albrecht Dürer who, at the close of the fifteenth century, took the meticulous art of woodcutting to a level that arguably has never been duplicated or surpassed. However, Julius Schnorr von Carolsfeld, a German who fell into the Nazarene movement of the early nineteenth century, certainly was talented in the gifts that God had given him. Carolsfeld's attention to detail was what gained him fame in the world of woodcutting.

In the selected woodcut for the Third Commandment, each day of creation is portrayed. Upon a closer look at this piece you can see the feet of God the Father resting on the world He created to remind the viewer that all has been placed under His feet. An even closer look draws the eye to the rest of God the Father as His eyes are closed. It is worth noting as well that the Father is covering His right hand with His left. The hand that is being covered is kept safe by the nature of the Father, for it is at His right hand that Christ will reign after the resurrection and ascension.

Christians now gather around the gifts of the Triune God every Lord's day for a respite. There, in the hallowed halls of Christ's house, we find rest from our sin only in the forgiveness of Christ Himself. Not unlike the father of the prodigal son, the master of all creation, who rested on the seventh day, watched as His children sold their birthright and inheritance to sinfully worship the idol of self.

Yet in this artwork, Christians see not only what is there, but also what is to come. As the father of the prodigal son made haste to run to his sin-broken son, so did the Triune God run to us through His Son's incarnation, death, and resurrection. Christ runs to us in baptism and in the Lord's Supper. Christ runs to us in the preached and inwardly digested word. That same Christ, who ran to us, did so to restore our inheritance and graft our names in the Lamb's book of life. So we flee to God's word every Sunday to hear the law and the gospel proclaimed, and we do not despise it, but give thanks for it, because it is by these means that we have a true hope within us.

In the name of the Father, and of the ✠ Son, and of the Holy Spirit.

God, our Father in heaven, who created all things and governs them with discipline and grace, grant us the wisdom to seek You face to face at the altar every Lord's Sabbath day of rest. May we be grateful to hear Your word, repent of our sins, and pray to You as our dear Father, until we find our final rest in You; through the Son and the Holy Spirit, one God, now and forever. *Amen.*

The Fourth Commandment

**Thou shalt honor thy father and thy mother
[that it may be well with thee and
thou mayest live long upon the earth].**

What does this mean?

We should fear and love God that we may not despise nor anger
our parents and masters, but give them honor, serve, obey, and
hold them in love and esteem.

Christ Taking Leave of His Mother was a popular subject during the fifteenth
and sixteenth centuries. Often in artistic portrayals, one can find Christ
blessing His mother as He takes His leave of her. This is not unlike the artistic
portrayal of Christ taking leave of us as He holds two fingers on His right
hand outward, while that same hand has been nailed to the cross. Christ
blessing us during His crucifixion is seen as a promise of what is to come
three days later. His benediction comes to its fullness as the tomb is emptied.

In Strigel's piece, one finds a different approach from Christ blessing His
mother. Instead, she holds tight to Christ as He comforts and consoles her
for what is to come. In a short time Christ will be released from Mary's grasp
and handed over to the guards to endure a mockery of a trial and soon pay
the price for her sins and for ours. In doing this, Christ honored His Father
in heaven and His mother, who clung to the cross.

This painting exposes an emotional wound of Christ's passion that is
largely overshadowed by His merits on the cross. However, we must also keep
in mind that because Christ was fully man and fully God, the separation
from His mother would have caused them both immeasurable emotional
pain and anguish. This point does not take away from Calvary—it adds to
the fullness of the suffering of Christ, just as it does also for Mary as she
heard the words of Simeon, "A sword shall pierce your own soul too."

Even amid this longing pain between mother and son, we find Christ
honoring His Father and His mother. As the angel Gabriel approached Mary
to deliver to her the message that she was with child by the Spirit to give
birth to the savior of the nations, she bent to the will of God. We read in
St. Luke that Mary exclaimed that it *"be unto me"* as a submission to the will
of God. This wasn't done begrudgingly or because she had no choice, rather
Mary was so joyful and articulate that her words are still confessed with
great fervor in the liturgical Lutheran church today. Since St. Mary carried

our Lord in the temple of her womb, all the generations have called her the most blessed among women, and the most fervent lover of the hope that is in Christ Jesus. May we, too, hold fast to the hope of the resurrection, and love and honor our parents as Christ loved and honored His.

In the name of the Father, and of the ⊹ Son, and of the Holy Spirit.

Lamb of God, You take away the sins of the world. Be with us each day as we strive to honor our fathers and mothers. May we find love in them through obedience and be reminded of the favor You found in Your Father's eyes by Your perfect sacrifice for us; for You live and reign with the Father and the Holy Spirit, now and forever. *Amen.*

Bernhard Strigel's *Christ Taking Leave of His Mother* (Circa 1520 AD)

The Fifth Commandment

Thou shalt not kill.

Peter Paul Rubens' *Cain Slaying Abel* (1608–1609 AD)

What does this mean?

We should fear and love God that we may not hurt nor harm our neighbor in his body, but help and befriend him in every bodily need [in every need and danger of life and body].

It is a tale nearly as old as time. Murder is the climax of hatred. Christ spoke to all Christians throughout generations when he said that having hatred for someone in your heart is to kill them. Yet before rejecting the realism pouring from Peter Paul Rubens' oil-on-panel rendition of Cain murdering his brother, let us all recall Christ's words, for all have murdered. Not only have all murdered, but all have also hurt, harmed, slandered, begrudged, and refused to help and care for their neighbors. Christ tells us that the next commandment to the greatest commandment is to love our neighbor as ourselves.

The reality of that pull and pang upon the sinner's conscience is what makes Ruben's piece all the more striking. Cain stands above his brother, club in hand. Note the horrified look on Abel's face. He looks up in such disbelief at his own brother's immense hatred. Abel's eyes are a mix of begging for mercy and utter astonishment at what is happening. We see that Cain will show no mercy on his brother, for his jealousy and loathing are simply too strong. This is depicted quite clearly in Cain's left hand grasping tightly around Abel's throat to cut off the breath of life that was breathed into their father. Here, the viewer can see true, unfiltered murder before anyone had even died.

"Do not kill" can seem like the easiest commandment to obey in the world. Yet all are guilty of murder simply because we have harmed our neighbor's body and have refused to help and care for our neighbor in his time of need. Good works for the Christian aren't merely in the form of not doing, but also in doing good to others. This commandment is directly tied to our Lord Jesus Christ, who was brought to His own death by those willfully breaking it. Our Lord was murdered, yet the blood that spilled from His death poured forgiveness, life, and salvation onto us. For this reason, we give thanks to God and pray that our hearts be turned from murderous thoughts.

In the name of the Father, and of the ☩ Son, and of the Holy Spirit.

Almighty God, You hate nothing You have made and forgive the sins of all who are penitent. Therefore, create and make in us contrite hearts, that by our lamenting of sins of hatred and murderous thoughts against our neighbor, we may receive from You, the God of all mercy, the remission so desired; through Jesus Christ, our Lord, who lives and reigns with You and the Holy Spirit, one God, now and forever. *Amen.*

The Sixth Commandment

Thou shalt not commit adultery.

What does this mean?

We should fear and love God that we may lead a chaste and decent life in words and deeds, and each love and honor his spouse.

Adultery in art always causes the eye to be drawn to the visual display of the depth to which humanity can descend into depravity of the soul. In Artemisia Gentileschi's piece, King David is shown lusting to such a degree that he becomes nothing more than a common voyeur. The dark shades and thick nature of the oil medium make King David's hiding in the shadows all the more sinister and self-serving.

Gentileschi was highly influenced by the masterful work of famed Italian painter Michelangelo Mersi da Caravaggio and her lines here represent this in her first work in the Neapolitan period. This is quite fortuitous, artistically speaking, as the oil and canvas bring out the darkness and lust that is found even in nobles. This stark painting reminds the Christian of the profound need for the forgiveness of sins through Jesus Christ.

Because of the admiration Christians have for King David, knowing that Christ would come from his lineage, we tend to want to be lenient with his immoral escapade. That is until the account is visually portrayed in such vivid detail that all pretense is washed away. What we see in this piece is that even the great king needed the forgiveness of his sins.

The biblical narrative doesn't simply stop at King David's lusting or even at his sleeping with Bathsheba, the wife of Uriah the Hittite. It tragically ends by King David so desiring Bathsheba that he sends Uriah to the front lines of the hardest fighting on the battlefield in hopes that Uriah would die and that he could take Bathsheba as his own. This evil plot was successful. Uriah was killed in battle and David took Bathsheba as his wife after her mourning. God was angered by King David's sin, for he had not lived an honorable, clean, and chaste life.

God expects us to live a clean and pure life, which becomes complete in the wondrous bond of Holy Matrimony. In the vows of marriage, man and wife are brought together and mystically become one. This oneness is not unique to marriage, but shows us the life of all Christians who are baptized into oneness with Christ. Therefore, all marriages are but a shadow of Christ the Bridegroom's marriage to His bride, the church.

In the name of the Father, and of the ✝ Son, and of the Holy Spirit.

Gracious Father, You care for Your creation and desire that men be fruitful and multiply. Therefore, guard our hearts and minds from the temptations of lust, fornication, and adultery; recall to our minds the blessed grace of Your Son, Jesus Christ, for in You we trust for all our desires of heart, mind, and body; through Jesus Christ, our Lord, who lives and reigns with You and the Holy Spirit, one God, now and forever. *Amen.*

Artemisia Gentileschi's *David and Bathsheba* (1636–1637 AD)

The Seventh Commandment

Thou shalt not steal.

What does this mean?

We should fear and love God that we may not take our neighbor's money or property, nor get them by false ware or dealing, but help him to improve and protect his property and business [that his means are preserved and his condition is improved].

While there is not much known about the author of the art for the Seventh Commandment, what is known is that there were many artists who were assigned to create the images of the Holman Bible. Like nearly all of the pieces in the Holman Bible from 1890, the style is that of a remade woodcut. While more crude and less detailed, this piece still gives an insight into the text of Isaac and Esau.

Isaac, the father of Esau and Jacob, had a taste for good food and a love of fine meat. This made Esau, who was a hunter by trade, his favorite son. Jacob preferred to stay in tents and work there. Since Jacob was the secondborn of the sons, Esau, being the oldest, had the prime birthright. Having the birthright meant that the older son would receive twice the inheritance of the younger brother.

One day, when Esau came into the tents, famished from hunting throughout the day, Jacob was able to persuade him to give Jacob his own birthright. Since this was done under the strain of extreme hunger, it is clear that Jacob received his brother's birthright under deceitful conditions. Therefore, the name Jacob will always mean "deceiver." Yet it is also clear that Esau despised his birthright and gave it up willingly for a mere meal. Similarly, we all have stolen and despised the gifts God has given to us.

Christ is the true birthright that is given to His holy people. In baptism, we are made heirs of His kingdom, and we are given a double portion of blessings as we close our eyes to this world and open them in the next. While Christians tarry in this world, they are brought together around the feast of the Lamb and eat sumptuously of the forgiveness of sins that is Christ's body and blood. Christians taste and see that the Lord is good and that His mercy endures for all eternity, for all sin.

Even Jacob, the deceiver, wrestled with Christ and refused to let go until the Lord blessed him. From that time forward, his name would be Israel, which means "to contend with God." Christians have contended with God as well. We were drowned in the baptismal waters until dead, and we have risen to life out of those same waters. Thanks be to God that we now live, not with a stolen inheritance, but with a legitimate inheritance through our rebirth in baptism into Christ.

In the name of the Father, and of the ✝ Son, and of the Holy Spirit.

O Christ, Lamb of God, You look upon Your servants with pity and love. In Your great mercy, forgive us our sins of stealing and desiring that which does not belong to us; for You live and reign with the Father and the Holy Spirit, one God, now and forever. *Amen.*

Illustration from the Holman Bible, *Esau Going for Venison* (1890 AD)

The Eighth Commandment

Thou shalt not bear false witness against thy neighbor.

What does this mean?

We should fear and love God that we may not deceitfully belie, betray, slander, or defame our neighbor, but defend him, [think and] speak well of him, and put the best construction on everything.

When the Pharisees spoke up against Jesus and claimed that they had Abraham as their father and that they had never been a slave to anyone (John 8), Jesus spoke a solid truth to them saying that the only way that men are free is by the truth. The Pharisees cried louder and louder that only Abraham was their father. To these claims Christ told them who their true father was: the devil.

The opposite of the truth is a deep and dark lie. There is no such thing as a little white lie. Humans move their mouths and the Lord speaks salutary words or the father of lies speaks. When the father of lies speaks, he speaks to kill. Christ went on to tell the Pharisees that if they had God as their father then they would love the Father's Christ, yet they spoke the words of their father, the devil. Woe to those who do the same.

Revelation tells a different story. It tells the story of the defeat of the dragon, who is the devil. The devil, with his demonic tribe of followers, battles with St. Michael the Archangel and other angels, and the devil does not prevail over them. He is cast out of heaven along with his satanic crew.

St. Michael is often portrayed in art as standing upon or over the dragon with a spear about to slay it, and often the spear is in the mouth of the dragon. In the illustration here, the spear has already plunged into the devil and it is notable that the spear is directly in the mouth of the dragon from which comes all of his lies. This story is retold in beautiful tempera and gold leaf on a panel that highlights the victory over the accursed devil.

May lies and deceit never be on the lips of the Christian, for when the Christian speaks lies, he sings in harmony with the father of lies. Rather let the Christian run to his true father, the Father who is in heaven, who from His Son, Jesus Christ, has rescued us from all ill and wrong.

In the name of the Father, and of the ✢ Son, and of the Holy Spirit.

O God, You in marvelous order send both angels and humans. Graciously grant that our life on earth may be defended by those who watch over us, that we be defended from the lies of the devil and speak only the truth of Your beloved Son; through the same Jesus Christ, Your Son, who lives and reigns with You in the unity of the Holy Spirit, one God, now and forever. *Amen.*

Master of Saint Verdiana's *Archangel Michael Slaying the Dragon*
(Circa 1380–1389 AD)

23

The Ninth Commandment

Thou shalt not covet thy neighbor's house.

What does this mean?

We should fear and love God that we may not craftily seek to get our neighbor's inheritance or house, and obtain it by a show of [justice and] right, etc., but help and be of service to him in keeping it.

The Prodigal Son is one of the most well known of Jesus' parables. It is a story of cashing in one's inheritance, living in horrific sin and degradation, then in contrition and repentance, and ultimately absolution and restoration. This parable is as heart-wrenching as it is beautiful. Nearly the entire text focuses on the younger of two brothers, who asked for his inheritance early and squandered it in horrid living. After losing it all and being forced to eat with the pigs, the youngest son decided he would return and confess his sins in the hope that he would be treated as well as a mere worker.

It is at this point in the story that we see the beauty of repentance and confession as it is met with absolution, forgiveness, and pure love from his father. The father, when he saw his son return from far off, went running after his son to forgive him. The younger son was broken, yet was restored with rings on his fingers, robes on his back, and the fatted calf killed to be eaten during a festival of reconciliation. Christians know that the angels rejoice when one sinner repents, yet the human heart can often turn hard when it doesn't sense what it determines to be fair.

The older brother was incensed that the younger brother was not only forgiven, but also seemed to be treated better than he was. Even worse, his father had never given him an animal to slay and eat while celebrating with his friends. It seemed to the older brother that he had kept the law of his father, and so he was the one who deserved the honor that his sinful brother was receiving. His heart turned to coveting his brother's new inheritance, given freely by the father who gave as he pleased from his own stores.

Christians also sinfully begrudge others their goods. These may include an inheritance or a house or a car or even the honor of one's family. Any of this begrudging is sinful and must be repented of with contrite hearts, with the sure and certain hope that our Father in heaven will hear and forgive us through His Son. Guercino's painting, using just oils, shows us the true nature of repentance and forgiveness. The father lovingly holds his son and the son weeps over his sins, but restoration is in the hands of his father and it is given in abundance. So it is with the Christian.

In the name of the Father, and of the ✝ Son, and of the Holy Spirit.

Lord Jesus Christ, You provide for all the needs and desires of this body and life. Grant all that I may need, and restrain me from falling into the temptation to covet that which does not belong to me, in order that I may be reminded that in You I have all that is needed and more, even the salvation of my soul; for You live and reign with the Father and the Holy Spirit, one God, now and forever. *Amen.*

Guercino's *Return of the Prodigal Son* (Circa 1651 AD)

The Tenth Commandment

Thou shalt not covet thy neighbor's wife, nor his man-servant, nor his maid-servant, nor his cattle, nor anything that is his.

What does this mean?

We should fear and love God that we may not estrange, force, or entice away our neighbor's wife, servants, or cattle, but urge them to stay and [diligently] do their duty.

For this work of art by Ingres, the focus is not on a biblical narrative, but a historical and fictionally dramatized one. It begs the question of how a narrative can be both a historical account and a fictional tale. It is for this reason that delving into the story of this painting can teach us a great truth regarding the Tenth Commandment.

Francesca da Rimini was a real person who lived between 1255 and 1285 AD. What brought her into infamy was her extramarital escapades. She was given away in marriage as a political peace offering to Giovanni Malatesta, who was lame and therefore undesirable to Francesca. Peace was made through the marriage until Francesca met Paolo, who was also married at the time. A sexual affair began between them that lasted for some ten years. What made the betrayal all the more treacherous was that Paolo was Giovanni's brother. The affair was suspected and eventually confirmed when Giovanni hid behind a curtain and caught the two in a sexual act.

Unfortunately for them all, they happened to be contemporaries of Dante Alighieri, who portrayed them in his masterful work, *Inferno*. In the fictional first volume, Dante and Virgil find Paolo and Francesca in the second circle of hell, which is reserved for the lustful. The scene and subsequent conversation find Dante in such a state of pity for them that he faints in despair.

While this tale is mixed with truth and fiction, it still holds that lusting after another's wife, servants, occupation, and so on, is not uncommon to history or to the hearts of Christians. In these moments of temptation, we fall to our knees and pray to Christ, "I am Yours, Jesus Christ. Lead me not into this temptation, but let me be content in the hope of my salvation."

In the name of the Father, and of the ✝ Son, and of the Holy Spirit.

O Holy Spirit, You enkindle in us a heart of pure faith in Christ and have given us a desire for the holy things of God. Grant us the pure desire to hear Your inspired word and to turn our hearts from the covetousness of another's wife, land, and possessesions, that we may find favor through Christ's death and resurrection alone; through You who lives and reigns with the Father and the Son, one God, now and forever. *Amen.*

Jean Auguste Dominique Ingres' *Paolo and Francesca* (1819 AD)

What Does God Say About These Commandments?

He says thus (Exodus 20:5 f.): I the Lord, thy God, am a jealous God, visiting the iniquity of the fathers upon the children unto the third and fourth generation of them that hate Me, and showing mercy unto thousands of them that love Me and keep My commandments.

What does this mean?

God threatens to punish all that transgress these commandments. Therefore we should dread His wrath and not act contrary to these commandments. But He promises grace and every blessing to all that keep these commandments. Therefore we should also love and trust in Him, and gladly do [zealously and diligently order our whole life] according to His commandments.

It comes as no surprise to Christians that God detests sin. From the fall into sin, there was subsequent punishment for transgressions. Adam was to work the fields by the sweat of his brow and Eve was to have pains in childbirth. Yet the worst of it all is that from the first sin through every subsequent sin, humans must die for their trespasses. Scripture teaches that the consequence of sin is that death comes to us all.

As Christians, we must take measure of our place according to the Ten Commandments and discover that having been weighed and measured we have been found wanting. Humanity cannot and will never be able to atone for its sinfulness. It is for this reason that the narrow chamber of the tomb waits for us all as a cold reminder of the horrors of our hearts and minds.

Have you honored your father and mother? Have you honored your pastor and those in authority over you? Have you loved your neighbor as yourself? Have you murdered in your heart or with your hands? Have you turned a lustful eye to another or another's wife? Have you stolen? We have broken all of God's Commands willingly. There is no hope in hopeless humanity.

Yet while we were still far off, Christ our Lord ran to us through His incarnation and nativity. In the Epiphany, all who have witnessed the miracles believed and pointed to Christ as the Father's Messiah. Christ taught and rebuked. Then He entered into Jerusalem, running to us once more, on a colt to turn His face to the cross. On the cross, Christ died for all our sins by taking the punishment that we so deserve. Yet the tomb could not hold Him. With Easter joy, all generations now proclaim that Christ is risen! We, who were doomed to die in our trespasses, now wait in the sure and certain hope of the second coming of our Lord and the resurrection of all the faithful.

We die; yet we live. The entire Ten Commandments were fulfilled in Christ. There is no greater joy than Easter joy. And that Easter joy is found in Christ as it is proclaimed before we partake in His flesh and blood by those in attendance, with angels, archangels, and all the company of heaven who laud and magnify Christ's holy name.

In the name of the Father, and of the ☩ Son, and of the Holy Spirit.

Hosanna. Save us, Christ, for we are Yours, and Yours alone. Instill in us true hearts and the joy of Easter morning. *Amen.*

The Promulgation of the Law in Mount Sinai
from *Figures de la Bible* (1728 AD)

THE CREED

*As the head of the family should teach it
in a simple way to his household*

**Flemish tapestry illustrating the first four articles [of twelve]
of The Apostles' Creed** (1475–1500 AD)

The First Article: Of Creation

**I believe in God the Father Almighty,
Maker of heaven and earth.**

What does this mean?

I believe that God has made me and all creatures; that He has given me my body and soul, eyes, ears, and all my limbs, my reason, and all my senses, and still preserves them; in addition thereto, clothing and shoes, meat and drink, house and homestead, wife and children, fields, cattle, and all my goods; that He provides me richly and daily with all that I need to support this body and life, protects me from all danger, and guards me and preserves me from all evil; and all this out of pure, fatherly, divine goodness and mercy, without any merit or worthiness in me; for all which I owe it to Him to thank, praise, serve, and obey Him. This is most certainly true.

God the Father as the creator of all things is a truth that, while incredible, is readily simple for Christians to profess and confess, making it easy to discount evolution in favor of creationism. Even Theistic Evolution, the heresy that claims that God created the world and set evolution in motion, doesn't hold water with the Christian. Yet the deeper that Christians climb into the text from Genesis and Luther's Small Catechism, the more the Holy Trinity unfolds before the faithful eye.

When God desired to create man, after He had created all that would sustain man, He spoke these words in Genesis 1:26: "*Let us make man in our image, after our likeness. And let them have dominion over the fish of the sea and over the birds of the heavens and over the livestock and over all the earth and over every creeping thing that creeps on the earth.*" The plural in the Hebrew text is not an accident. Father, Son, and Holy Spirit desired to make man in their image, yet it was the image of the Father that was the will for mankind. In other words, image can be defined as God's will. This was wonderful, yet it remained only as we were without sin. Once Adam and Eve fell into sin, humanity was in such a state that our will became our own will and was no longer the natural will of God. This was the great lie that Satan, the deceiver, told to Eve and which was told to Adam. Satan promised them that they would be like God, knowing both good and evil. What they didn't realize, however, was that not knowing evil was the blessing of all blessings.

Even after the fall of mankind and the subsequent casting out of man from the Garden of Eden, God still preserved them. It was by the sweat of

Adam's brow that soil was seeded, yet God grew the plants and sustained the lives of Adam and Eve and their children to this very day. It is in this joy that we give thanks and gladly confess that God has created us and has given us all that we take for granted each day. God not only gives us food and drink and clothing and shelter, but He also provides us with the mirror of His great love for the church in our marriages and children.

Why does God the Father do this for us? For the same reason that He created us and provides for us out of His abundant love for us. This is summarized well in John 3:16–17: God loved us so much that He sent His Son to die and be raised again that we would believe in Him.

In the name of the Father, and of the ☩ *Son, and of the Holy Spirit.*

O God, You are the Father of all that is created. Grant us a noble heart to thank, praise, and obey You and Your Son Jesus Christ; who lives and reigns with You and the Holy Spirit, one God, now and forever. *Amen.*

Woodcut by Hans Brosamer for the 1550 Frankfurt Edition of the Small Catechism of Martin Luther

The Second Article: Of Redemption

And in Jesus Christ, His only Son, our Lord; who was conceived by the Holy Ghost, born of the Virgin Mary; suffered under Pontius Pilate, was crucified, dead, and buried; He descended into hell; the third day He rose again from the dead; He ascended into heaven, and sitteth on the right hand of God the Father Almighty; from thence He shall come to judge the quick and the dead.

What does this mean?

I believe that Jesus Christ, true God, begotten of the Father from eternity, and also true man, born of the Virgin Mary, is my Lord, who has redeemed me, a lost and condemned creature, purchased and won [delivered] me from all sins, from death, and from the power of the devil, not with gold or silver, but with His holy, precious blood and with His innocent suffering and death, in order that I may be [wholly] His own, and live under Him in His kingdom, and serve Him in everlasting righteousness, innocence, and blessedness, even as He is risen from the dead, lives and reigns to all eternity. This is most certainly true.

Распятый Иисус Христос
Viktor Vasnetsov's *Crucified Jesus Christ* (1885–1896 AD)

St. Paul boldly wrote to the Corinthians, "*For I decided to know nothing among you except Jesus Christ and Him crucified. And I was with you in weakness and in fear and much trembling, and my speech and my message were not in plausible words of wisdom, but in demonstration of the Spirit and of power*" (1 Corinthians 2:3–4). With these words, pastors throughout Lutheranism have strained and struggled to find the purity in which to speak of Christ's atoning sacrifice on the cross of Calvary. Pastors are called to proclaim Christ crucified for the forgiveness of sins, for it is at the sacrifice into which we are baptized that the image of God was placed back onto sinful humanity. We were reconciled to the Father through the all-availing work of the begotten Son on the cross of Calvary.

Still, there is cause to back up and recall Christ's incarnation. Christians must remember what brought Christ down to a world marred with sin. Paul Gerhardt put it best in his hymn, "O Lord How Shall I Meet Thee": "Love caused Thy incarnation, love brought Thee down to me; Thy thirst for my salvation procured my liberty. Oh, love beyond all telling, that led Thee to embrace, in love all love excelling, our lost and fallen race!" Here, Gerhardt masterfully sums up the entire second article of the Creed.

It was in Christ's coming down to earth that we find the lengths that God would go to rescue us from remaining east of Eden. The God of Gods and Lord of Lords was knitted in the womb of His mother just as all humanity was, and it was for one purpose that stands out above all reasoning and explanation: Christ "thirsted for our salvation," "procured our liberty" through His death, and brought us, the "lost and fallen race," into the favor of the Father through His own precious and adorable blood.

However, no tomb could hold the love of Christ and so He arose the third day, sealing the eternal tomb from Christians that we would not die the eternal death of Hell. Christ burst forth from the tomb in glorious victory, which we proclaim. By this victory, we live with Christ by grace through faith in Him. In this truth no part is small. In Him there is only the body of Christ, the church, who gathers around His true body and blood at the altar to partake in His most Holy Supper. The body and bride of Christ, the church, is washed cleanly into the death and resurrection of Christ that she would have true life. So, she does.

In the name of the Father, and of the ✝ Son, and of the Holy Spirit.

Lord Jesus Christ, Lamb of God, You look down from heaven and behold Your washed people clothed in righteousness and sipping the cup of blessing that overflows with Your blood. Grant us a right heart to confess You; for you live and reign with the Father and the Holy Spirit, one God, now and forever. *Amen.*

The Third Article: Of Sanctification

**I believe in the Holy Ghost; one holy Christian Church,
the communion of saints; the forgiveness of sins;
the resurrection of the body; and the life everlasting. Amen.**

What does this mean?

I believe that I cannot by my own reason or strength believe in Jesus
Christ, my Lord, or come to Him; but the Holy Ghost has called me
by the Gospel, enlightened me with His gifts, sanctified and kept me
in the true faith; even as He calls, gathers, enlightens, and sanctifies
the whole Christian Church on earth, and keeps it with Jesus Christ
in the one true faith; in which Christian Church He forgives daily
and richly all sins to me and all believers, and at the last day will
raise up me and all the dead, and will give to me and to all believers
in Christ everlasting life. This is most certainly true.

In baptism we are given the true faith. St. Peter records his confession of
what happens in baptism when he writes for all to believe:

> *For Christ also suffered once for sins, the righteous for the unrighteous, that
> he might bring us to God, being put to death in the flesh but made alive in
> the spirit, in which he went and proclaimed to the spirits in prison, because
> they formerly did not obey, when God's patience waited in the days of Noah,
> while the ark was being prepared, in which a few, that is, eight persons, were
> brought safely through water. Baptism, which corresponds to this, now saves
> you, not as a removal of dirt from the body but as an appeal to God for a good
> conscience . . . (1 Peter 3:18–21)*

For the orthodox Christian, these words from St. Peter are very hard to get
around. In fact, the only way to face his confession of baptism is to venture
headlong through it and into the waters of Holy Baptism. In baptism, we
are granted the same wonderful blessing given to Noah and his family. We
are saved by the same waters that drown the evilness of our hearts. Baptism
brings us out of the Red Sea and onto dry ground.

The reality of this faith was shown in great abundance on the day of
Pentecost. The book of Acts records, *"When the day of Pentecost arrived, they
were all together in one place. And suddenly there came from heaven a sound
like a mighty rushing wind, and it filled the entire house where they were
sitting. And divided tongues as of fire appeared to them and rested on each one
of them"* (Acts 2:1–2). When those holy words were written, they recorded the

beginning of the church of Christ. From that fascinating day of Pentecost to today, the Holy Spirit has continued to pour out the true faith that is given by the perfect grace of our Lord, Jesus Christ.

The church of Christ remains on this earthly realm for the sake of the Holy Spirit, who gives us that which we need most. The Holy Spirit gives us all that we need and preserves us through the very faith He gives us. For this, Christians must be thankful for the work of the Holy Spirit and pray to Him to increase faith in us daily.

In the name of the Father, and of the + *Son, and of the Holy Spirit.*

O Holy Spirit, You enkindle a burning faith in our hearts and minds. Be with us now, for the hour of our Lord draws near. Grant us peace and patience as we await Christ's return in judgement; remind us of the perfect faith that you placed in our hearts the day we were baptized, and bring it to its final rest in our last hour, that we might sing the praises of the Triune God now and in the world to come; for You live and reign with the Father and the Son, one God, now and forever. *Amen.*

Spiritus Hos Edocens, Linguis Hic Ardet Et Igne (Circa 980–993 AD)

THE LORD'S PRAYER

*As the head of the family should teach it
in a simple way to his household*

Jean Pénicaud III's *Triptych with the Lord's Prayer* (Circa 1560–1575 AD)

Introduction

Our Father who art in heaven.

What does this mean?

God would thereby [with this little introduction] tenderly urge us to believe that He is our true Father, and that we are His true children, so that we may ask Him confidently with all assurance, as dear children ask their dear father.

In the Gospel of Matthew, Christ our Lord prays to His Father, who is also our Father, with these words,

> "I thank you, Father, Lord of heaven and earth, that you have hidden these things from the wise and understanding and revealed them to little children; yes, Father, for such was your gracious will. All things have been handed over to me by my Father, and no one knows the Son except the Father, and no one knows the Father except the Son and anyone to whom the Son chooses to reveal him. Come to me, all who labor and are heavy laden, and I will give you rest. Take my yoke upon you, and learn from me, for I am gentle and lowly in heart, and you will find rest for your souls. For my yoke is easy, and my burden is light." (Matthew 11:25–30)

These beautiful words are the very backbone that allow Luther's introduction to stand up straight with full confidence: when we come to our Father who is in heaven, He hears us as His own dear children. Referring to God as our Father was unheard of during the time of Jewish rule and law. In many parts of Scripture, Pharisees and Sadducees alike would claim others as their father. The preeminent father was Abraham, yet Christ clearly teaches His disciples that those who know the Son also know the one who sent the Son; for Christ alone knows the Father, yet through Christ's glory and merit we are made children of the Father.

In Hans Brosamer's woodcut, published in the 1550 Frankfurt edition of Luther's Catechism, he makes a very clear distinction without using words, relying completely on the art. Notice in his piece that Christ is teaching all those who have ears to hear, learn, and inwardly retain the greatest of all prayers. Each man has his hands folded in beautiful reverence as he also prays with Christ. This reverence is compounded in the double genuflection (kneeling) of every man, yet Christ stands as the mediator pointing to the Father who is portrayed in the top left corner as He gazes upon His Son and His children from His heavens. Christians would do well to burn this image in their minds as they reverently pray to our Father in heaven who sent His

Son to take on our ills, sins, and burdens to replace them with His yoke, which is easy and light.

Woodcut by Hans Brosamer of Christ teaching the disciples the Lord's Prayer from the 1550 Frankfurt Edition of the Small Catechism of Martin Luther

In the name of the Father, and of the ✝ Son, and of the Holy Spirit.

Blessed and most Holy Father in heaven, You bring us into Your family through Your Son, Jesus Christ. Grant that we remember and rejoice in our baptismal grace that You have poured over us, bringing faith into our hearts by the Holy Spirit; through Jesus Christ, our Lord, who lives and reigns with You and the Holy Spirit, one God, now and forever. *Amen.*

The First Petition

Hallowed be Thy name.

What does this mean?

God's name is indeed holy in itself; but we pray in this petition that it may become holy among us also.

How is this done?

When the Word of God is taught in its truth and purity, and we as the children of God also lead holy lives in accordance with it. To this end help us, dear Father in heaven. But he that teaches and lives otherwise than God's Word teaches profanes the name of God among us. From this preserve us, heavenly Father.

In a single image brushed by mere oil on panel, Jan Cornelisz Vermeyen captures a great realization of what the holiness of God the Father is through our sight and imagination. It is clear by the title of the painting that the central subject of this piece was to be a depiction of the most Holy Trinity. Yet a closer examination of this piece shines forth a great reminder from the prophet Isaiah that the one who is most holy dwells in the heavens and also with contrite humanity through the incarnation of God's Son, and through the Holy Spirit, dwells with the lowly in spirit.

Regarding the Father's holiness, Isaiah records,

> *For thus says the One who is high and lifted up, who inhabits eternity, whose name is Holy: "I dwell in the high and holy place, and also with him who is of a contrite and lowly spirit, to revive the spirit of the lowly, and to revive the heart of the contrite. For I will not contend forever, nor will I always be angry; or the spirit would grow faint before me and the breath of life that I made. Because of the iniquity of his unjust gain I was angry, I struck him; I hid my face and was angry, but he went on backsliding in the way of his own heart. I have seen his ways, but I will heal him; I will lead him and restore comfort to him and his mourners, creating the fruit of the lips. Peace, peace, to the far and to the near," says the Lord, "and I will heal him." (Isaiah 51:15–19)*

Certainly the first words from the lips of God the Father acknowledge God's high and holy place; then He continues regarding His anger that is fierce yet abating through His great love for His creation and for His Son, Jesus Christ. While this text does not strictly speak of Christ, similarities abound in the turning away of the Father's face, as He did before Christ proclaimed that God had forsaken Him. Still yet, Christ was healed on the third day, the mourners of Christ's death were comforted, and Christ's lips brought peace to the disciples in the closed room and peace both near and far.

The beautiful painting from Vermeyen brings all of this to the forefront of the observer. There in the middle is God the Father with the world under His feet, while all around Him you see the angels carrying away the instruments of Christ's death, leaving the Son of God upon the lap of the Father with the Holy Spirit ready to descend on that wonderful day of Pentecost. The most beautiful aspect of this piece is in the Father breaking through the fourth wall with His eyes on the observer. God, with His gaze, says, "Out of my Holiness, this all is for you, my children."

In the name of the Father, and of the ✝ Son, and of the Holy Spirit.

Most Holy Father, You did not spare even Your own Son, that we might be reconciled to You. Pour out Your love into our hearts through Your Spirit, that we may truly give thanks to You for Your holy deeds and love for us in making us Your own; through Jesus Christ, who lives and reigns with You and the Holy Spirit, now and forever. *Amen.*

Jan Cornelisz Vermeyen's *The Holy Trinity* (First half of the sixteenth century)

The Second Petition

Thy kingdom come.

What does this mean?

The kingdom of God comes indeed without our prayer, of itself; but we pray in this petition that it may come unto us also.

How is this done?

When our heavenly Father gives us His Holy Spirit, so that by His grace we believe His holy Word and lead a godly life here in time and yonder in eternity.

In the Apostle's Creed, we confess before God and one another that we believe that Christ will come again to judge "both the living and the dead." Scripture speaks this truth often, yet many go searching for the answers in St. John's

Stefan Lochner's *Last Judgment* (Circa 1435 AD)

Revelation, though *"Thy kingdom come"* is found in many other areas of Scripture, including the Gospel of St. John. John records for the church, *"Do not marvel at this, for an hour is coming when all who are in the tombs will hear his voice and come out, those who have done good to the resurrection of life, and those who have done evil to the resurrection of judgment"* (John 5:28–29).

In Lochner's detailed depiction of Christ's second advent, the observer's eye is drawn to either the bottom left or the bottom right after identifying Christ, St. Mary, and St. John. To the right there is a brutal rushing and clamoring amongst the demonic horde, whose only desire is to reap those whose lives have been led in wickedness. This is juxtaposed with the saints on the left who are gently being ushered into the mansion that has been prepared for them by Christ Himself. In this imagery we find a dividing line that runs down the center of the painting. The righteous are fought over tooth and nail by the angels, who are gathering them together for the bliss of heaven. Yet there are those who are being dragged off to hell by hoards of demons, many still trying to cling to the eartly treasures they adored.

Why would a Lutheran Christian desire that day of judgment, awaiting it with joy and anticipation? Why would Lutherans pray that this kingdom would come if it means that we may be pulled by our own horns into hell? Luther has answered this beautifully as he catechizes us that it is the Holy Spirit given by the Father, that by His grace alone we believe His holy word and live godly lives on this earth and, in the perfection that has been prepared for us through Jesus, in the next.

God's kingdom comes daily even without our prayers through His holy word, in baptism and the Lord's Supper, yet we are still called to pray. In those prayers we check our stores of oil and the Lord trims our wicks for the final coming, when God the Father will look at us through the eyes of His Son and say to us, "You have been faithful over a little; I will set you over much. Enter into the joy of your master."

In the name of the Father, and of the ✝ Son, and of the Holy Spirit.

Lord Jesus Christ, You show great love for Your people who have traveled through the Red Sea of Your Holy Baptism, and You hear and answer our prayers. Place on our lips a true and right confession of You, that we may live godly and pleasing lives; through You who lives and reigns with the Father and the Holy Spirit, one God, now and forever. *Amen.*

The Third Petition

Thy will be done on earth as it is in heaven.

What does this mean?

The good and gracious will of God is done indeed without our prayer; but we pray in this petition that it may be done among us also.

How is this done?

When God breaks and hinders every evil counsel and will which would not let us hallow the name of God nor let His kingdom come, such as the will of the devil, the world, and our flesh; but strengthens and keeps us steadfast in His Word and in faith unto our end. This is His gracious and good will.

Masaccio's *Christ in the Garden of Gethsemane* (1424–1425 AD)

"Not my will, but Thy will be done." Nearly every Christian has prayed this outside of the Lord's Prayer. As pious as it is to pray this prayer after the intercessions are completed, our sinful hearts still desire that the luck of the roll will eventually land on our will. Yet when this plea is placed within the Lord's Prayer, there is heavenly context that precedes these words. That context is that the petitioner has just prayed that Christ's kingdom would come soon. The one praying is asking Christ to come to earth to judge the living and the dead, yet each time this is prayed, the will of God is that you are sustained and loved without the final coming of Christ. So, the Christian continues to wait.

In Scripture, as the Passion of our Lord draws ever closer, we find Christ in the Garden of Gethsemane on His knees looking up into the heavens praying to His Father. St. Matthew records, *"Going a little farther, he fell with his face to the ground and prayed, 'My Father, if it is possible, may this cup be taken from me. Yet not as I will, but as you will.'"* In those words, Christ is asking the Father in perfect submission that the cup of wrath that He must drink would be passed along, for the task of saving every repentant, baptized sinner was much greater than any pastor has ever been able to convey to his people.

The result of the prayer from Christ has been beautifully portrayed in Masaccio's *Christ in the Garden of Gethsemane*. In dark oil tones on wood, Masaccio portrays the answer to the request from Christ. The answer was the Father's will would be done. The angel in the portrait would not dare to touch the cup of wrath he was handing to Jesus for even the slightest touch would be too much for the angel. The angel covers his hands in his vestment and delivers the answer to Christ's petition. This cup must be consumed by only one; the Holy Christ. This was for our sake. With pious hands, Christ drank deeply from the cup at His crucifixion.

We, who are not Christ, pray these words with great care, realizing that the will of God our Father will always be done. The Christian is confident in the knowledge that His will shall be done, yet we fervently pray that the same will of God would also be done amongst us here in the church militant. In that fight here on earth we can be assured that our heavenly Father will, for our sake, break and hinder the desires of the devil as he has been defeated by Christ's death and resurrection.

In the name of the Father, and of the ✠ Son, and of the Holy Spirit.

Holy Father, You gaze upon us from Your blissful and heavenly realm. Hear us as we pray Your will to be done among us, that we be defended from all evil; through Your Son, Jesus Christ, our Lord, who lives and reigns with You and the Holy Spirit, one God, now and forever. *Amen.*

The Fourth Petition

Give us this day our daily bread.

What does this mean?

God gives daily bread, even without our prayer, to all wicked men; but we pray in this petition that He would lead us to know it, and to receive our daily bread with thanksgiving.

What is meant by daily bread?

Everything that belongs to the support and wants of the body, such as meat, drink, clothing, shoes, house, homestead, field, cattle, money, goods, a pious spouse, pious children, pious servants, pious and faithful magistrates, good government, good weather, peace, health, discipline, honor, good friends, faithful neighbors, and the like.

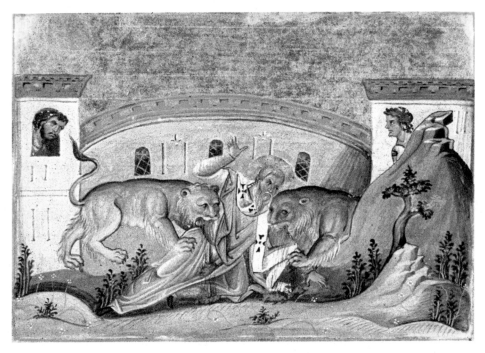

Anonymous' *Ignatius of Antioch* (Pre-seventeenth century AD)

Eating is one of the small joys in life, even though eating is necessary for survival. Even in the pre-fall Garden of Eden, there was an abundance of lush foods given by God. After the fall, Adam was made to work the ground, yet it was still God who provided the food, though now the food is given to the righteous and unrighteous alike, even without a prayer. God does desire that we recognize that our food comes from His holy hand and that we pray to be reminded of this daily.

Luther hits the nail on the head when he remarks that when God gives us our daily bread it includes all that we need to sustain this body and life. God didn't rest there with only giving us nourishment for the day. He gave over His Son, Jesus Christ, to be our true bread and true drink. John professes Christ as the true food as he records in chapter 6, *"I am the bread of life; whoever comes to me shall not hunger, and whoever believes in me shall never thirst."* Our Father in heaven gives us not only our daily bread so that we would live to see tomorrow, He gives us the true flesh of Christ that we would live everlastingly.

In receiving the flesh of the Son of Man, we stand firm in the face of death and proclaim, "Here I am, O death, I have a Lord who has given me my everlasting needs. Do your worst!" In the anonymous painting of St. Ignatius of Antioch there is no doubt that the depiction is gruesome. But what led up to this gruesome and evil act was a true and right confession of Christ. He wrote to his brothers and sisters, "May nothing entice me till I happily make my way to Jesus Christ! Fire, cross, struggles with wild beasts, wrenching of bones, mangling of limbs—let them come to me, provided only I make my way to Jesus Christ."

When the time came for St. Ignatius to be martyred for the faith, he proclaimed a pure understanding of daily bread. He wrote, "Let me be food for the wild beasts, for they are my way to God. I am God's wheat and shall be ground by their teeth so that I may become Christ's pure bread." In these words we find a faith that is unyielding. St. Ignatius was sustained by the bread that lasts forever. He gladly became God's wheat to be crushed in the jaws of the lions so that he would finally be with Christ.

In the name of the Father, and of the ✠ Son, and of the Holy Spirit.

Lord Jesus Christ, You give bread to the righteous and unrighteous alike. We pray that You not only give us our daily bread that sustains us for a day, but grant that we yearn for the bread that is Your flesh that leads to everlasting life so that when our time of dying comes, we may be made one with You according to the promise given in the Eucharist that we will live, even though we died; through You, who lives and reigns with the Father and the Holy Spirit, now and forever. *Amen.*

The Fifth Petition

And forgive us our trespasses, as we forgive those who trespass against us.

What does this mean?

We pray in this petition that our Father in heaven would not look upon our sins, nor deny such petitions on account of them; for we are worthy of none of the things for which we pray, neither have we deserved them; but that He would grant them all to us by grace; for we daily sin much, and indeed deserve nothing but punishment. So will we verily, on our part, also heartily forgive and also readily do good to those who sin against us.

"Lord, how many times shall I forgive my brother or sister who sins against me? Up to seven times?" Some form of this question has entered the mind of every Christian. This time in the Gospel of Matthew it was Peter who asked

Anton Robert Leinweber's *Peter's Denial* (Before 1921 AD)

the question of Christ. The question came on the heels of Christ teaching the disciples about reconciling sinners in the church. We also glimpse the first words of Christ regarding the office of the keys when He proclaims, *"whatever you bind on earth will be bound in heaven, and whatever you loose on earth will be loosed in heaven."* This loosing of sins is no small matter to the church and it would become the whole world to Peter.

Soon Peter would commit the very sin that he swore he would never commit against Jesus. *"And again he denied it with an oath: 'I do not know the man.'"* To every Christian these words are unfathomable, yet they are deeply ingrained in our hearts when we are called to confess Christ in a world that He told us would hate Him. Do we know the man? Do we proclaim Him as the one true Son of God? When we deny Him by omission, we deny Him. There, at that time, the Law works upon our hearts to turn us from our wickedness back to the cross of Christ.

In Anton Leinweber's work on Peter's denial, he portrays the pure heartbreak of Peter as he realizes that the cock's crow signaled his ultimate betrayal of Christ. Away from the pressures of those who were calling him a Christian, he hides his face from God and himself as the true evil of his trespass against Christ weighs heavily on his heart. Who could forgive such an evil act of betrayal? Is there even any hope of forgiveness? When we slay one another with our words and our actions, we drive a spike in marriages, families, and friendships. Peter's deeds drove an even deeper wound into Christ, as we all have. Those devilish tools used to torture our Lord, those nails that pierced His hands and feet, and the spear that expelled the sacraments of blood and water from Christ's side were all for the forgiveness of the betrayers of God Himself. Who could forgive these things?

Jesus asked Peter, "Do you love me?" and he said to him, "Lord, you know everything; you know that I love you." Jesus said to him, "Feed my sheep." With these words Jesus restored Peter from his sins. He was free from all his sins and he was commissioned to feed Christ's church. In Christ, there is forgiveness.

In the name of the Father, and of the ☩ Son, and of the Holy Spirit.

Christ, our Lord, You reign over Your church and have forgiven us much. Grant that we forgive others as You have forgiven us; for You live and reign with the Father and the Holy Spirit, one God, now and forever. *Amen.*

The Sixth Petition

And lead us not into temptation.

What does this mean?

God, indeed, tempts no one; but we pray in this petition that God would guard and keep us, so that the devil, the world, and our flesh may not deceive us, nor seduce us into misbelief, despair, and other great shame and vice; and though we be assailed by them, that still we may finally overcome and gain the victory.

William Blake's *The Temptation and Fall of Eve*
(1808 AD illustration of Milton's *Paradise Lost*)

The tempter is great at his job. Satan will go to any length to attack Christians where their greatest desires of the heart lie. He is a genius at supplying the mortar to help us build our own idol that looks exactly like us. In the Gospel of St. Matthew, Christ was driven out into the wilderness where He was to be tempted. Christ had fasted for forty days and forty nights, so Satan first tempted Christ with food. He then took Christ up to the top of the temple and tempted Him through His divinity saying, *"If You are the Son of God, throw Yourself down from here,"* for the angels were meant to protect the Messiah. Finally, Satan offered Christ the whole world if He would only bow down and worship him. What is amazing is what Christ used to refute His tempter. Each time a temptation came, Christ quoted the word of God to Satan, for it is the word of God that Satan cannot stand. Even the demons knew Christ as the word made flesh and trembled at His presence among them.

In William Blake's *The Temptation and Fall of Eve*, he conveys a truth that is rarely discussed among Christians. Satan makes sin look like beautiful buildings that are enticing to enter, yet behind the façade, there is merely a whitewashed tomb prepared for the dead.

This simple work craftily brought to life through pen and watercolor on paper shows Eve's fall as but a sweet kiss from the serpent. This killer kiss is separated only by the fruit that Eve so desires for herself. When she saw the fruit, she knew that it looked good for eating, yet it was Satan who tempted her into sin, claiming that she would be like God if she ate it. Once her teeth broke the skin of the fruit, the only kiss that was left was the kiss of death. The serpent in Blake's work is shown coiled around Eve, entangling her in her own sin and death. What a costly kiss that was.

It is certainly true that where God builds a church, the devil builds a chapel. These temptations wouldn't be temptations if they didn't seem desirable to benefit the idol of self. Christians know that God Himself does not tempt us, yet we are still called to pray that God would keep us out of the entanglement of the serpent's coils. The Christian is called to deny himself rather than make himself an idol. Christians are to live in this wretched world, yet we have been set apart by our baptism into Christ's death and resurrection. Christians are called to pray that we would not be tempted, so that on the day of our dying, the only kiss we will receive is the kiss of peace from Christ Himself.

In the name of the Father, and of the ☩ Son, and of the Holy Spirit.

O Christ, You fulfilled the whole Law on our behalf and won victory over Satan. Keep us from all temptation that, escaping all danger, we may appear with You in Your kingdom; for You live and reign with the Father and the Holy Spirit, one God, now and forever. *Amen*

The Seventh Petition

But deliver us from evil.

What does this mean?

We pray in this petition, as in a summary, that our Father in heaven would deliver us from all manner of evil, of body and soul, property and honor, and at last, when our last hour shall come, grant us a blessed end, and graciously take us from this vale of tears to Himself into heaven.

Where God's presence is, there too, is His promise. From Genesis 3 on, fallen humanity has had an everlasting promise that we would be delivered from evil. After mankind fell into sin, God the Father looked at the serpent, who believed he had won the greatest victory, and the Father spoke, *"I will put enmity between you and the woman, and between your offspring and her offspring; he shall bruise your head, and you shall bruise his heel"* (Genesis 3:15).

This promise from God the Father was not merely a threat to Satan, it was a promise to him and a promise for us. There would come a day when Satan and all his works and all his ways would be put under the feet of the Son of God. This day would come to us on Good Friday when Christ took onto Himself the sins of the whole world and three days after, rose again to life for the sake of the whole world. In other words, on that day, evil was delivered the greatest blow.

It is through the holy waters of baptism that we were brought into the death of Christ and brought out of those waters as Christians with a faith and heart to love all that God has given us. It was in the words, "I baptize you in the name of the Father, and of the Son, and of the Holy Spirit" that we were delivered from the evil one and claimed as God's own child.

For this reason, many Christians make the sign of the cross at these words at the Invocation during the Divine Service as a remembrance of their baptism. Making the sign of the holy cross is a pious way of confessing the reality that is in Christ's baptismal promise when we recall those words first spoken in the waters of baptism. Likewise, it is meet, right, and salutary for Christians to make the sign of the holy cross at the words, "deliver us from evil" in the Lord's Prayer, for the same words that recall our baptism in the Invocation also apply in our deliverance from evil.

And still the Christian prays that our Father in heaven would keep us from all evil and guide and guard our hearts and minds by His Holy Spirit.

We pray that this would be to us in this body and life, so that when our time of dying comes, we would be delivered into heaven where we will see God's promise with our own eyes and not another's, as Job declared. The Christian who dies in faith and hope dies well, having been delivered by the Father, and the Son, and the Holy Spirit.

In the name of the Father, and of the ✝ Son, and of the Holy Spirit.

Almighty Father, You have created all things for our benefit and sustenance. Be with us each day by Your Holy Spirit, that we may be kept from temptations of the flesh, from all evil and assaults from the evil one, and the world that hates Your word, in order that we may one day leave this world that is veiled in the tears of sin and death and live with You; through Jesus Christ, who lives and reigns with You and the Holy Spirit, now and forever. *Amen.*

Hieronymus Bosch's *Christ Crowned with Thorns* (1479–1516 AD)

Cima da Conegliano's *God the Father* (1510–1517 AD)

Amen.

What does this mean?

That I should be certain that these petitions are acceptable to our
Father in heaven and heard; for He Himself has commanded us so
to pray, and has promised that He will hear us. Amen, Amen; that is,
Yea, yea, it shall be so.

*"So if the Son sets you free, you will be free indeed. I know that you are offspring
of Abraham; yet you seek to kill me because my word finds no place in you. I
speak of what I have seen with my Father, and you do what you have heard
from your father."* With these words in John 8, Christ cuts to the quick the
Jews who were listening to Him. Christ knew that the Jews saw Abraham as
their father, for it was the Triune God who raised Abraham up to his place
of Abraham the Father. Yet Christ, who is the truth and the very Word of

God per John 1, was telling these men the truth that the Father was not known in this world until Christ's incarnation. When Christ was rejected, so the Father was rejected. Abraham longed for the day of Jesus, yet the Jews rejected the one for whom Abraham awaited.

Christ then says to them, *"If God were your Father, you would love me, for I came from God and I am here. I came not of my own accord, but he sent me. Why do you not understand what I say? It is because you cannot bear to hear my word."* To love the Father is to love his Word. To love the Father's Word is to love the Son. And to love the Son is to love the Father. There can be no disconnect between God's Word and God's Son, for they are the same. Yet this was missed by the Jews and they desired to kill the Son rather than bear the truth.

The truth in St. John, chapter 8, reinforces the beauty in the Lord's Prayer. For the Christian, the mere fact that we can call God our Father is a baptismal miracle. The allowance of this would have been a most fantastical dream for the Jews. Yet the rejection of the cornerstone was absolute. Christians are not only allowed to call God our Father, but through the truth of Christ we are called to call God our Father as a proclamation of the truth that is in us.

Luther still says it best when we read and inwardly digest his words in the Small Catechism, ". . . I should be certain that these petitions are acceptable to our Father in heaven and heard; for He Himself has commanded us so to pray, and has promised that He will hear us." Christians have the pure comfort that God our Father hears the prayers of His own beloved children and that those prayers are righteous in His sight. All of this is done through the intercession of the Son of God, who has claimed us as His own. Yes, yes, this is most certainly true for the Christian redeemed by the blood of the Lamb.

In the name of the Father, and of the ✠ Son, and of the Holy Spirit.

Our Father, who art in heaven, grant us firmly to trust in the redemption of Your Son, that with thankful lips we may confess that in Him is the "Yes" and the "Amen"; through the same Jesus Christ, our Lord. *Amen.*

THE SACRAMENT OF HOLY BAPTISM

*As the head of the family should teach it
in a simple way to his household*

Leonardo da Vinci's *Baptism of Christ* (Circa 1475 AD)

First

What is Baptism?

Baptism is not simple water only, but it is the water comprehended in God's command and connected with God's Word.

Which is that word of God?

Christ, our Lord, says in the last chapter of Matthew: *Go ye into all the world and teach all nations, baptizing them in the name of the Father, and of the Son, and of the Holy Ghost.*

Pietro Longhi's *The Baptism* (1755 AD)

Baptism is the cornerstone of faith in and through Christ Jesus. Luther reminds us in this first part of the article on Holy Baptism of what St. Matthew wrote, *"Go therefore and make disciples of all nations, baptizing them in the name of the Father and of the Son and of the Holy Spirit, teaching them to observe all that I have commanded you."* Many apt theologians have held that the translation of the Greek word for "nations" can (and perhaps should) be translated as "Gentiles." This interpretation changes the perspective of this phrase and reminds us that the disciples weren't simply sent to reach across lines in the sand that we call nations, but rather to go to all peoples to bring them into the church by the means of water and the word of God.

In Pietro Longhi's painting, the Christian can see exactly who "all nations" and "all Gentiles" truly are. In glorious beauty and artistry, Longhi points directly toward the infant in the midst of becoming a Christian through this means of God's grace. Even the light contrasting the darkness illumines the reality of baptism into the ark that is the church. In the same Gospel of St. Matthew, he records Christ as saying, *"Let the little children come to me and do not hinder them for the kingdom of heaven belongs to such as these."* Indeed, these waters, placed in connection with God's word, are the gateway into the kingdom of heaven. What parents would not desire this most supreme gift for their child? Luther and the early church believed these matters to be of the highest order and that they could not be bought with silver or gold. Only in Christ's death do we find true and holy recompense in and through God.

Yet the human and fallen mind asks, "How is this possible?" Even more beautifully drawn together than our painting, Christ answers this for us. St. Matthew records the words of Christ, *"All authority in heaven and on earth has been given to me."* "What then," the world asks, "did Christ do with the authority given to Him from the Father?" And Christ answers directly with the Great Commission to "Go" to those nations and Gentiles with water and the word of God. The world may scoff at this, but for the Christian it is the very power of God to forgive and adopt mortal flesh and to graft that flesh into the body of Christ.

In the name of the Father, and of the ✠ Son, and of the Holy Spirit.

Heavenly Father, You do not reject those who come to the holy waters under Your authority given to Your blessed Son. Look upon us who are baptized and grant us the true peace in this blessed sacrament. We also pray that You will look upon those who are to be baptized and grant them Your divine protection until the day they are sealed into the ark by Your holy hand; through Your Son, Jesus Christ, we pray. *Amen.*

Secondly

What does Baptism give or profit?

It works forgiveness of sins, delivers from death and the devil, and gives eternal salvation to all who believe this, as the words and promises of God declare.

Which are such words and promises of God?

Christ, our Lord, says in the last chapter of Mark: *He that believeth and is baptized shall be saved; but he that believeth not shall be damned.*

The word of God clearly declares that baptism saves sinners from their sins. The Gospel of St. Mark professes, *"Whoever believes and is baptized will be saved, but whoever does not believe will be condemned."* Yet it is not until St. Paul's words that we understand how this blessed and unspeakable gift becomes a reality for the sinner. In his letter to the Romans, he writes,

> *Do you not know that all of us who have been baptized into Christ Jesus were baptized into his death? We were buried therefore with him by baptism into death, in order that, just as Christ was raised from the dead by the glory of the Father, we too might walk in newness of life.* (Romans 6:3–4)

Baptism is intimately linked and founded in the death and resurrection of Christ. Outside of the atonement won for us by Christ on the cross, there is no baptism, and without baptism, the assurance of our resurrection from the dead remains but dry bones in a dark valley of sin. Christ in His mercy went to the cross for our sake to rescue us from everlasting death. St. Paul records once again to the Romans,

> *For if many died through one man's trespass, much more have the grace of God and the free gift by the grace of that one man Jesus Christ abounded for many. And the free gift is not like the result of that one man's sin. For the judgment following one trespass brought condemnation, but the free gift following many trespasses brought justification.* (Romans 5:15–16)

This justification is found at the cross of Christ, our Lord. In baptism, the Christian travels from the cross to the grave, from the grave to the resurrection, and we await the coming of the same Christ who ascended into heaven. Baptism in Christ's death trims the wick of our lamp as we await the coming of the bridegroom. We are cleansed and prepared, yet wait with anticipation as we gather together in Christ's church to receive the true blessings of Christ.

We have been buried and raised with Christ through our baptism. The end result of such a journey to and through the font means that we are set apart; we are the wheat and the sheep. In the pain and anguish of that tortuous device from which our Lord did hang, we find the most beautiful salvation that the devil and his minions can never overcome. Because of this beautiful and wondrous act of our Lord, we are set free from the power of the devil, and have crowns waiting for us in heaven. This is our claim. This is our baptism.

In the name of the Father, and of the + Son, and of the Holy Spirit.

O Lord Jesus Christ, You faithfully tend Your sheep and rescue us from sin, death, and the devil. Remind us daily of Your promise in our baptism, that we may walk in newness of life; for You live and reign with the Father and the Holy Spirit, one God, now and forever. *Amen.*

El Greco's *Christ on the Cross* (Unknown)

Thirdly

How can water do such great things?

It is not the water indeed that does them, but the word of God which is in and with the water, and faith, which trusts such word of God in the water. For without the word of God the water is simple water and no baptism. But with the word of God it is a baptism, that is, a gracious water of life and a washing of regeneration in the Holy Ghost, as St. Paul says, Titus, chapter three: *By the washing of regeneration and renewing of the Holy Ghost, which He shed on us abundantly through Jesus Christ, our Savior, that, being justified by His grace, we should be made heirs according to the hope of eternal life. This is a faithful saying.*

Viktor Vasnetsov's *The Baptism of Saint Prince Vladimir* is one of the most recent artistic examples used to illustrate the faith. Though the fresco is recent, the story it tells is anything but new. By 980 AD, Prince Vladimir had gathered for himself the Kievan Rus' realm that would eventually come to include everything from the Baltic Sea to the Black Sea. His power was immense and his influence as a professed pagan was unquestionable. Vladimir went as far as to erect statues of pagan gods, keep eight hundred concubines, and he was successful in spreading paganism.

Around the year 987 AD, Vladimir sent out envoys to different religious areas. Talks with Muslims, Jews, Catholics, and Eastern Orthodox leaders commenced for but a short period as Vladimir was drawn to the beauty of the divine liturgy of the Eastern Orthodox. Vladimir was baptized into the Christian faith and took a single wife. While the reason for the baptism has been argued, there can be no doubt of the regeneration shown through the great deeds of Vladimir. He tore down all the pagan idols, built many churches and cathedrals, professed his faith, and would practice the faith by great and constant acts of charity and love for his people.

Vladimir is still celebrated as a saint in many church bodies; however, the Lutheran celebrates the faith given to him in Holy Baptism. Lutherans do not see baptism as a mere symbol of what the person already believes. Rather Lutherans view all Trinitarian baptisms as regenerative and renewing of a right spirit. St. Paul wrote these words to St. Titus:

for we ourselves were once foolish, disobedient, led astray, slaves to various passions and pleasures, passing our days in malice and envy, hated by others and hating one another. But when the goodness and loving kindness of God our Savior appeared, he saved us, not because of works done by us in righteousness, but according to his own mercy, by the washing of regeneration and renewal of the Holy Spirit. (Titus 3:3–5)

That hope that is within us springs from the regeneration of the Holy Spirit, bringing us into faith in Jesus and love for one another. This truth is no small thing and it goes well beyond the world's understanding that Christianity calls us to be nice. No, we are called by the Spirit to true faith and to love our neighbors as ourselves.

In the name of the Father, and of the ✝ Son, and of the Holy Spirit.

O Holy Spirit, You have called us to faith and hope in Christ. Grant that our faith might bear fruit in keeping with repentance; for You live and reign with the Father and the Son, one God, now and forever. *Amen.*

Viktor Vasnetsov's *The Baptism of Saint Prince Vladimir* (1890 AD)

Fourthly

What does such baptizing with water signify?

It signifies that the old Adam in us should, by daily contrition and repentance, be drowned and die with all sins and evil lusts, and, again, a new man daily come forth and arise; who shall live before God in righteousness and purity forever.

Where is this written?

St. Paul says in Romans, chapter 6: *We are buried with Christ by Baptism into death, that, like as He was raised up from the dead by the glory of the Father, even so we also should walk in newness of life.*

It is an unfortunate truth that there is no new heresy under the sun. That is not to say that old heresies are not repackaged, gift wrapped, and presented as a free gift from heretical churches. For this reason one must look closely at Luther's words in this section of Holy Baptism. Luther confesses, "It signifies that the old Adam in us should . . . ." Luther's usage of the word *signify* is not the same as *symbol*. Some Christians have happily thrown the leaven of heresy into the lump of God's word regarding baptism. The addition of the phrase, "baptism is a symbol of an inward faith," clearly contradicts what Christ spoke regarding baptism, Christ raising the dead, and disregards the writings of St. Paul on the subject of baptism.

Luther continues, "It signifies that the old Adam in us should, by daily contrition and repentance, be drowned and die with all sins and evil lusts, and, again, a new man daily come forth and arise." Here is a life and death confession of what baptism is, as well as what and why Luther used the word *signify*. Through all that follows this word, the most clear truth is that baptism comes before daily contrition, that the Old Adam in us drowns and dies daily, and after that death we arise a new man every morning as baptized Christians. The signal is not a goal to reach before the sacraments, but reminds us, like a car blinker, that we have been baptized and that we have been called to repent and believe and trust in our baptism into Christ.

Luther quotes St. Paul in this section of the Small Catechism when he writes, "We are buried with Christ by Baptism into death, that, like as He was raised up from the dead by the glory of the Father, even so we also should walk in newness of life." In Lucas Cranach's piece, we find an imaginative scenario where Luther and others from the Reformation are watching Christ raise Lazarus from the dead. This paints a beautiful picture for the Christian as well. We, who have been grafted into Christ through baptism, are painted into the portrait of Jesus' crucifixion and we bear witness to His resurrection. Why? Because we have died and risen again with Him in those holy waters of baptism. Thanks be to God that we are clean.

In the name of the Father, and of the ✝ Son, and of the Holy Spirit.

Blessed Holy Spirit, You sanctify every life in the waters of Holy Baptism. Grant that we remember with wonder what was begun in us in that most holy sacrament so that we may live godly lives of good deeds toward our neighbors and be daily awaked to the truth that we have died with Christ and have risen with Him as well; through You who lives and reigns with the Father and the Son. *Amen.*

Lucas Cranach the Elder's *Luther with Jesus Raising Lazarus* (1518 AD)

CONFESSION

How Christians should be taught to confess

Pietro Longhi's *The Confession* (Circa 1750 AD)

What is Confession?

Confession embraces two parts: the one is, that we confess our sins; the other, that we receive absolution, or forgiveness, from the confessor, as from God Himself, and in no wise doubt, but firmly believe, that our sins are thereby forgiven before God in heaven.

The sheer brilliance of Albrecht Dürer's work in almost every medium has already been discussed, particularly in his woodcuts. This woodcut of King David is a stark contrast to what Martin Luther taught. It is known that Luther would flagellate himself as punishment and to achieve a proper level of penance or repentance, but one needs to keep in mind the time period from which this woodcut was created. In 1510, Luther had not posted his famous Ninety-Five Theses on the castle door, let alone added his other faithful reforms.

Still, this woodcut shows us a glimpse into the overburdened heart. It comes rather naturally that we would desire to punish ourselves for our sins, yet punishment is not repentance. Flagellation is not contrition. Punishment is not ours to carry out on ourselves when Christ saw fit to rescue us from our sins.

Punishment such as beating ourselves to a pulp (physically and mentally) stands in stark contrast to what is being taught in the Confession section of Luther's Small Catechism. Why? Because we know, trust, and believe that a confession of our sins has not one part, but two. These parts are rather simple: that we would confess our sins and that we would receive absolution by a trusting faith.

Lutheran Christians have practiced private confession and absolution since before the momentum of the Reformation began. It is a trustworthy practice to confess our sins to our pastor and hear him absolve us with the very words of God. For those who disregard private confession, consider the words of 1 John,

> If we say we have no sin, we deceive ourselves, and the truth is not in us. If we confess our sins, he is faithful and just to forgive us our sins and to cleanse us from all unrighteousness. If we say we have not sinned, we make him a liar, and his word is not in us.

These words are not easy words to read and even more difficult to digest, yet Christians are called to confess their sins and hear the beautiful forgiveness of Christ. Confession should never be considered a must, but it is a special comfort given for those who "in no wise doubt . . . but firmly believe that our sins are thereby forgiven before God in heaven."

Albrecht Dürer's *King David Doing Penance* (1510 AD)

In the name of the Father, and of the ☩ Son, and of the Holy Spirit.

Heavenly Father, You have promised to hear all of our prayers, petitions, and intercessions. We pray that You send Your Holy Spirit to enkindle in our hearts contrition and repentance, that the fruit of our repentance be most assuredly met with Your Son's faithful forgiveness of our sins; for You live and reign with the Son and the Holy Spirit, one God, now and forever. *Amen.*

What sins should we confess?

Before God we should plead guilty of all sins, even of those which we do not know, as we do in the Lord's Prayer. But before the confessor we should confess those sins alone which we know and feel in our hearts.

The human mind can be a terrible place to hang one's hat. The mind is capable of and inclined toward all types of evil thoughts and desires. Often, even after asking our gracious Lord for forgiveness, the mind will lend its ear to the devil so he might whisper, "Yes, you believe that you are forgiven, yet who would forgive such a horrible sin that you have committed?" Our mind's response to this is to remember the horrid things we have done against our neighbors and against the God who created us. In our solitary hours or in the hour of our deepest darkness we remember just what wickedness we have brought to this world and to those who love us.

In John chapter 6, after our Lord told His followers that if they would not eat of His body and drink of His blood they would have no life in them, many, if not most, of them left Him because they could not bear the words of our Lord. These men rejected what Christ was offering them for they sought something else. Even though our Lord intimately connected the eating of His flesh, faith in Him, and the resurrection of the dead on the last day, they left for greener pastures in a different shepherd's barren field.

When this happened, Christ turned to His twelve disciples and asked them if they, too, wanted to go away from Him. Peter answered Him with the words that should be on our lips daily. *"Lord, to whom shall we go? You have the words of eternal life and we have believed, and have come to know, that you are the Holy One of God."* Yet even Peter would betray our Lord. After the resurrection, our Lord restored Peter and laid upon his confession the keys of the pastoral office to bind and loose the sins of Christ's own flock.

When the devil whispers to your mind that you are not good enough or that your sins are far too great to forgive, confess your sins to your pastor, that you might hear with your own ears the loosening of your bonds of sin. The keys have been handed down for the assurance and comforted conscience of the sinner. These keys, held by faithful undershepherds of Christ, open the gates of heaven through Christ's own absolution. Our piece by Pietro shows this well as the unworthy sinner, Peter, receives that which frees the flock to graze in the Lord's field forever.

Confession

In the name of the Father, and of the ✠ Son, and of the Holy Spirit.

Christ, our Lord, You forgive us freely from the bondage of our sin and guilt. Grant that we be terrified by our sins, but also flee to the one to whom we should go; quicken our feet to run to Your gracious forgiveness, even when spoken through the lips of sinful men; for You live and reign with the Father and the Holy Spirit. *Amen.*

Pietro Perugino's *Christ Handing the Keys to St. Peter* (1481–1482 AD)

73

Which are these?

Here consider your station according to the Ten Commandments, whether you are a father, mother, son, daughter, master, mistress, a man-servant or maid-servant; whether you have been disobedient, unfaithful, slothful; whether you have grieved any one by words or deeds; whether you have stolen, neglected, or wasted aught, or done other injury.

All sin is an attempt to dethrone the Lord, our God. We desire this seat for ourselves—to make for ourselves idols of our own flesh and blood, rather than the gold that was used to construct the calf in Genesis chapter 32. The fact is that to break any Commandment is to break all the Commandments, especially the First Commandment. If this were not so we would still be centered comfortably in the great Garden of Eden instead of wallowing in the muck just to the east of Eden. Adam and Eve bought into Satan's lie that they *"would be like God, knowing both good and evil."* And since that horrid time, God the Father has burned hot in anger against our sins.

The Lord spoke to Moses, *"I have seen this people, and behold, it is a stiff-necked people. Now therefore let me alone, that my wrath may burn hot against them and I may consume them, in order that I may make a great nation of you"* (Exodus 32:9–10). Truly we are a stiff-necked people going to and fro, spreading our idolatry until God's anger burns hot. To this point, we are to constantly consider our station by making use of the Ten Commandments.

Luther tells us to ask ourselves, ". . . whether you are a father, mother, son, daughter, master, mistress, a man-servant or maid-servant; whether you have been disobedient, unfaithful, slothful; whether you have grieved any one by words or deeds." These are the questions that we should ask ourselves, and by asking them, find that we are in desperate need of respite from the wrath of God. We find this respite in that God the Father poured out His hot anger and wrath onto His Son, Jesus Christ, our Lord, on the cross of Calvary.

In Rembrandt's marvelous work of Moses breaking the Tablets of the Law, we find a shadow of the hot anger of God on the face of Moses. Even after Moses pleaded with God to not pour out His anger on the people of Israel, Moses broke the Tablets after seeing the idols that were built, and he destroyed the idol of the golden calf in his anger. The Lord, out of His great love, poured out His anger and wrath on His Son so that we would be His true children and He our true Father. As His children, we confess our sins and expose our guilt, that He would gaze upon us through the eyes of His crucified and risen Son, and forgive us of all our trespasses.

Rembrandt's *Moses Smashing the Tablets of the Law* (1659 AD)

In the name of the Father, and of the ☩ Son, and of the Holy Spirit.

Almighty God, who gave the Law through Moses, by that same Law show us the horror of our lovelessness toward God and neighbor, and grant us true contrition, that by the gospel we may turn to you for the forgiveness of sins; through Jesus Christ, our Lord, who lives and reigns with You and the Holy Spirit, one God, now and forever. *Amen.*

Pray, propose to me a brief form of Confession.

You should speak to the confessor thus: Reverend and dear sir, I beseech you to hear my confession, and to pronounce forgiveness to me for God's sake.

Proceed!

I, a poor sinner, confess myself before God guilty of all sins; especially I confess before you that I am a man-servant, a maidservant, etc. But, alas, I serve my master unfaithfully; for in this and in that I have not done what they commanded me; I have provoked them, and caused them to curse, have been negligent [in many things] and permitted damage to be done; have also been immodest in words and deeds, have quarreled with my equals, have grumbled and sworn at my mistress, etc. For all this I am sorry, and pray for grace; I want to do better.

A master or mistress may say thus:

In particular I confess before you that I have not faithfully trained my children, domestics, and wife [family] for God's glory. I have cursed, set a bad example by rude words and deeds, have done my neighbor harm and spoken evil of him, have overcharged and given false ware and short measure.

And whatever else he has done against God's command and his station, etc.
   But if any one does not find himself burdened with such or greater sins, he should not trouble himself or search for or invent other sins, and thereby make confession a torture, but mention one or two that he knows.
   Thus: In particular I confess that I once cursed; again, I once used improper words, I have once neglected this or that, etc. Let this suffice. But if you know of none at all (which, however is scarcely possible), then mention none in particular, but receive the forgiveness upon your general confession which you make before God to the confessor.

Then shall the confessor say:

God be merciful to thee and strengthen thy faith! Amen.

Furthermore:

Dost thou believe that my forgiveness is God's forgiveness?

Yes, dear sir.

Then let him say:

As thou believest, so be it done unto thee. And by the command of our Lord Jesus Christ I forgive thee thy sins, in the name of the Father and of the Son and of the Holy Ghost. Amen. Depart in peace.

But those who have great burdens upon their consciences, or are distressed and tempted, the confessor will know how to comfort and to encourage to faith with more passages of Scripture. This is to be merely a general form of confession for the unlearned.

Pompeo Batoni's *The Return of the Prodigal Son* (1773 AD)

THE SACRAMENT
OF THE ALTAR

*As the head of the family should teach it
in a simple way to his household*

Evangelical Lutheran Church Liturgy and Sacraments
Brandenburg St.-Nikolai-Kirche, Gemälde

What is the Sacrament of the Altar?

It is the true body and blood of our Lord Jesus Christ, under the bread and wine, for us Christians to eat and to drink, instituted by Christ Himself.

Unknown Artist's *Man of Sorrows between Angels* (Circa 1470 AD)

Man of Sorrows is a work of art that has been mostly forgotten by the major populous of the world, yet was (and still is) the center of Reformation for a fading group of Christians in Prague. This painting still hangs in Prague and was one of the most crucial works of art during the Bohemian Reformation.

Today, it is doubtful that anyone could gaze upon the painting and not be struck with some type of emotional response. It is not easy to look upon as it shows with graphic detail what Christ went through to save us from our sins. Yet even if one looks past the blood and the gore, the forlorn face of Christ, the crown of thorns, and everything else, the most graphic and intimate detail of the painting is the chalice catching the blood and Christ tearing off His own flesh to give for true food.

It is not surprising that this painting may be offensive to some. After all, our sinful flesh and Satan desire us to consider Christ apart from the sufferings of the cross. Yet we must constantly remind ourselves of what Christ has done for us, which includes us eating and drinking His body and blood so that we would have life within us that leads to everlasting life. The reality depicted in *Man of Sorrows* is hard to look at, just as it was also hard to hear Jesus even speak about our eating His flesh and drinking His blood. As previously mentioned, in John chapter 6, many of the Jews heard Christ speak of this forthcoming meal and they, along with many of Jesus' disciples, went away from Jesus because the concept was too difficult to understand.

Jesus says in John chapter 6, *"This is the bread that came down from heaven, not like the bread the fathers ate, and died. Whoever feeds on this bread will live forever. . . . When many of his disciples heard it, they said, 'This is a hard saying; who can listen to it?'"* This bread that we eat and the wine that we drink is not like what we find in the supermarket, and the cost for us to receive this gift was infinitely higher. The Jews were not incorrect in their question to Jesus; they simply did not believe what He was saying. Now, after the bloody mess and death that we see in *Man of Sorrows*, we can better understand the cost of what we freely receive. As Luther wrote, "It is the true body and blood of our Lord Jesus Christ." Not only is He the gift, but He is the gift-giver as well.

In the name of the Father, and of the ✝ Son, and of the Holy Spirit.

Lord Jesus Christ, who in Your dying woes looked down upon us with compassion, grant us faithfully to flee to Your body and blood, given and poured out for us for the forgiveness of our sins; for You with the Father and Holy Spirit are one God, now and forever. *Amen.*

Where is this written?

The holy Evangelists, Matthew, Mark, Luke, and St. Paul, write thus:

Our Lord Jesus Christ, the same night in which He was betrayed, took bread: and when He had given thanks, He brake it, and gave it to His disciples, and said, Take, eat; this is My body, which is given for you. This do in remembrance of Me.

After the same manner also He took the cup, when He had supped, gave thanks, and gave it to them, saying, Take, drink ye all of it. This cup is the new testament in My blood, which is shed for you for the remission of sins. This do ye, as oft as ye drink it, in remembrance of Me.

Vicente Juan Masip's *The Last Supper* (1562 AD)

Leonardo Di Vinci's *Last Supper* is a marvelous work of art and has rightly been fawned over for centuries. However, there is much to be said for Vicente Juan Masip's work of the same name that better highlights Luther's Small Catechism. Masip is able to portray Christ during His Last Supper, making the Eucharist as the central item in the painting. While Masip is drawing our eyes to the Eucharist, he does so by refusing to separate the Eucharist from

Christ's own body with a simple placing of the left hand of Jesus on His chest, elevating the Eucharist with His right hand. Masip paints every eye in the painting (save one) as fixed on the Eucharist instead of on the face of Christ as an aesthetical proclamation that both are the same substance. Where Christ suffered, died, and merited our salvation through His body and blood being poured out on the cross, likewise that same body, blood, and merit that is poured out from the cross is poured onto the paten and into the chalice.

As Christ spoke the words, *"This is my body, which is given for you. Do this in remembrance of me,"* He was speaking plainly for all to know that the Eucharist is His own flesh given for the forgiveness of sins. In the same way, when Christ speaks, *"This cup that is poured out for you is the new covenant in my blood,"* He isn't speaking metaphorically to confuse the hearers of these words; rather Christ used plain words to point to a magnificent truth; Christ is Holy Communion.

What Luther's Sacrament of the Altar instills in the diligent reader is that the words of Jesus are not merely worth noting, but that they are what they say they are, and they do what they say they do. Therefore, when Christ says, *"For the forgiveness of your sins,"* we must be able to believe that with the same assurance that we would believe that Christ is truly present in Holy Communion.

Luther refuses to cherry pick the words of Jesus on the one hand by saying, "Christ is not present, though He says those words," and then on the other hand say, "Jesus really does forgive your sins." Both statements are equally true because their merits are based on the one who is speaking them. Therefore, we must take Jesus at His word that Holy Communion is His body and blood, just as we must take His word that we have His forgiveness. Christ and His merits can never stand alone outside of the promise and fulfillment in the Word of God Himself, who is Jesus.

In the name of the Father, and of the + *Son, and of the Holy Spirit.*

Lord Jesus Christ, You revealed Yourself in the flesh knitted together in the womb of St. Mary. We pray that you reveal Yourself in the true flesh and blood in Your sacrament of the altar for the forgiveness of our sins and for the salvation of our souls; for You live and reign with the Father and the Holy Spirit. *Amen.*

What is the benefit of such eating and drinking?

That is shown us in these words: *Given, and shed for you, for the remission of sins;* namely, that in the Sacrament forgiveness of sins, life, and salvation are given us through these words. For where there is forgiveness of sins, there is also life and salvation.

Unknown Illuminator's *The Crucifixion on Detached Leaf*
(Fifteenth century AD)

"For where there is forgiveness of sins, there is also life and salvation." These words from Martin Luther have the largest impact for the Christian in a short phrase. Not only do these words ring true for the sacrament of the altar, but also everywhere that forgiveness is spoken and resides as the balm for the overburdened consciences of those who confess their sins. Where there is faith, there Christ is and remains, offering to the sinner forgiveness, and where forgiveness is, there also is Christ, who grants us life and salvation. To run down the logic of Luther's statement here is nothing less than pure comfort for the sinner. Luther does not say, "Where you have enough good works, there is also life and salvation." For we are justified by grace through faith and our works are for the benefit of our neighbor.

Why then would Christ choose to give us His body and blood as a means in which grace is bestowed on the sinner? Is baptism not enough? Is pastoral absolution not enough? Let us consider how intimate the task of eating truly is. Men court young ladies under candlelight over a good meal. Husbands and wives enjoy meals together and as they do, they share the kitchen table in unity. Moreover, when children enter the picture, the table and meal becomes a familial event shared over food that is lovingly prepared by the parents to nourish their children. Each of these examples are instances of passionate intimacy as expressed through the meal.

Likewise, the sacrament of the altar has been lovingly prepared by the Father sending His Son to die for His bride, the church. As the church that is wedded to Christ, we are brought into a familial meal. However, it is not fried chicken that is passed to the bride or her children, nor is it a symbolical meal where the family is asked to use their imaginations to consume the meal. Rather, it is the meal of the true body and blood of our Lord and master. The question should never be, "Isn't another means of grace enough?" as to pit one means against the other as if they were separate graces. It is enough that Christ told us to eat and drink because we are His very own, and by His wounds our meal is prepared. The catch of the day is the forgiveness of sins, and where there is the forgiveness of sins, there is also life and salvation.

Look closely at the wine the angels are collecting from Christ in the unknown artist's work. They are collecting the blood of Christ from His own body to be especially given to you. Let us flee to the altar of the Lord.

In the name of the Father, and of the ✠ *Son, and of the Holy Spirit.*

Christ, Lamb of God, You take away the sin of the world. Have mercy on us, forgive us, and move us to eat and drink of Your holy body and blood to the forgiveness of our sins and to the salvation of our souls; for You live and reign with the Father and the Holy Spirit. *Amen.*

How can bodily eating and drinking do such great things?

It is not the eating and drinking, indeed, that does them, but the words which stand here, namely: *Given, and shed for you, for the remission of sins.* Which words are, beside the bodily eating and drinking, as the chief thing in the Sacrament; and he that believes these words has what they say and express, namely, the forgiveness of sins.

Sandro Botticelli's *The Last Communion of St. Jerome* (Circa 1495 AD)

St. Jerome once famously quoted Virgil when he said, "On all sides round horror spread wide; the very silence breathed a terror on my soul." In this short sentence, we find an eloquent summation of hell. St. Jerome knew of the terrors of hell and feared for his own soul. He also surrounded himself with many books for formative catechesis. It wasn't his studies that saved his soul, yet he was passionate about catechizing himself as much as he could before he entered heaven.

Every Christian father should have this desire, not only for himself, but more importantly for his children. Fathers should know a glimpse of hell so that they would usher their children into formative catechesis and get them to the sacrament of the altar as soon as possible. Why? Because the Great Physician has given us the medicine for everlasting life through His body and blood.

In this scene we find that all of the stops have been pulled out for St. Jerome's last communion. The priest is fully vested, the altar boys hold the candles high, and two monks are aiding Jerome in kneeling to receive Christ. Let us remember that this was an extremely learned man and diligent priest, and a man of great charity. Yet he is clad with nothing but dingy sleep attire; the very clothes in which he would die. Those clothes highlight that this person, regardless of his station, still begs to taste of the Lord's body and blood for the last time in his earthly life. Lutherans would do well to learn from this piece of art by Botticelli. On the last day of our earthly life, it is the phrase, "Given and shed for you for the remission of sins" that makes all the difference in the world.

This art suggests that a pastor should vest for Holy Communion even in the home; then how much more so for the Divine Service! Pastors should have pious men and children aiding them in the holy work of God.

After all, we all wear dying men's clothes, yet the Lord has the words of eternal life, and He is the one to whom the burdened are to go. In death and life there is the body and blood of our Lord that has been given and shed for us. May we, who wear the clothes of a dead man, forever trust in the words of the Lord that all the shedding of His blood and the body that was broken are His true words, and that when we eat and drink, we remember that it is the word of God and the Son of God that we are consuming.

In the name of the Father, and of the ☩ Son, and of the Holy Spirit.

O Christ, You have given us Your body and blood for the forgiveness of our sins. Grant us to firmly believe that it is the forgiveness of sins, life, and salvation; for You live and reign with the Father and the Holy Spirit. *Amen.*

Who, then, receives such Sacrament worthily?

Fasting and bodily preparation is, indeed, a fine outward training; but he is truly worthy and well prepared who has faith in these words: *Given, and shed for you, for the remission of sins.*

But he that does not believe these words, or doubts, is unworthy and unfit; for the words *For you* require altogether believing hearts.

In the fourth chapter of St. Matthew's Gospel, we find that Christ is led by the Holy Spirit out into the wilderness to be tempted by the devil. In Juan de Flandes' piece, we see only the temptation of the stone to be turned to bread, thus proving that Jesus is the Christ. We do well to focus our attention on the fact that it is the devil holding the stone to tempt Christ in Flandes' work and recall who is the true bread of life given by the hand of the pastor.

The Gospel reads, *And after fasting forty days and forty nights, he was hungry. And the tempter came and said to him, "If you are the Son of God, command these stones to become loaves of bread." But he answered, "It is written, 'Man shall not live by bread alone, but by every word that comes from the mouth of God'"* (Matthew 4:2-4).

Luther records for us in this section of his Small Catechism that "Fasting and bodily preparation is, indeed, a fine outward training." Christ Himself fasted in preparation for the temptation, and we are asked by Luther to keep in mind that fasting and bodily preparation to receive the holy sacrament is a salutary endeavor for the Christian to practice. However, those who are to worthily receive the sacrament of the altar are not those who place their trust in the outward training of the body, but who firmly believe that when Christ says, "given and shed for you, for the remission of your sins," that we take our Lord at His word. Likewise, those who are unfit for the sacrament of the altar are those who doubt that Christ is present in the sacrament. This does, of course, exclude the one who would dare to place an "if" before "you are the Son of God," whether he be the devil or a pagan.

Christ announces to the devil that he has failed to tempt Christ with these simple words, *"Man shall not live by bread alone, but by every word that comes from the mouth of God."* This is most certainly true for us as well. Yet Christ does not speak these words to ward us away from Him, but to draw us nearer to Him. We live by the word of God and not by bread alone. We receive the word of God in the awfully needed law and gospel from our faithful pastors. We receive faith in that word of God in the font at baptism. It is also God's word found in the flesh and blood of Christ and not in stone nor some self-sustaining magic trick. That word of God is for us. May we not neglect it, but firmly believe Jesus' word about it in His own sacrament of the altar.

In the name of the Father, and of the ✝ Son, and of the Holy Spirit.

Christ, our Lord, You call us to come to the sacrament and we come. May we firmly believe Your words regarding the holy sacrament and eat our fill of Your grace and deeply drink of Your mercy in that sacrament; for You are the only true Word of God, and it is in Your name that we pray. *Amen.*

Juan de Flandes' *The Temptation of Christ* **[The Stones]** (Circa 1500 AD)

DAILY PRAYERS

How the head of the family should teach his household to pray morning and evening

Marco Basaiti's *Christ On The Mount of Olives* (1510 or 1516 AD)

Morning Prayer

In the morning, when you rise, you shall bless yourself with the holy cross and say:

In the name of God the Father, Son, and Holy Ghost. Amen.

Then, kneeling or standing, repeat the Creed and the Lord's Prayer. If you choose, you may, in addition, say this little prayer:

I thank Thee, my heavenly Father, through Jesus Christ, Thy dear Son, that Thou hast kept me this night from all harm and danger; and I pray Thee to keep me this day also from sin and all evil, that all my doings and life may please Thee. For into Thy hands I commend myself, my body and soul, and all things. Let Thy holy angel be with me, that the Wicked Foe may have no power over me. Amen.

Then go to your work with joy, singing a hymn, as the Ten Commandments, or what your devotion may suggest.

Ebenezer Newman Downard's *Morning Prayer* (1860–1861 AD)

Evening Prayer

In the evening, when you go to bed, you shall bless yourself with the holy cross and say:

In the name of God the Father, Son, and Holy Ghost. Amen.

Then, kneeling or standing, repeat the Creed and the Lord's Prayer. If you choose, you may, in addition, say this little prayer:

I thank Thee, my heavenly Father, through Jesus Christ, Thy dear Son, that Thou hast graciously kept me this day, and I pray Thee to forgive me all my sins, where I have done wrong, and graciously keep me this night. For into Thy hands I commend myself, my body and soul, and all things. Let Thy holy angel be with me, that the Wicked Foe may have no power over me. Amen.

Then go to sleep promptly and cheerfully.

Anna Ancher's *Evening Prayer* (1888 AD)

*How the head of the household should teach his household
to ask a blessing and return thanks*

Hans Baldung Grien's *The Trinity and Mystic Pietá* (1512 AD)

Asking a Blessing

The children and servants shall go to the table with folded hands and reverently, and say:

The eyes of all wait upon Thee, O Lord; and Thou givest them their meat in due season; Thou openest Thine hand, and satisfiest the desire of every living thing.

Then the Lord's Prayer, and the prayer here following:

Lord God, heavenly Father, bless us and these Thy gifts, which we take from Thy bountiful goodness, through Jesus Christ, our Lord. Amen.

Fritz von Uhde's *Das Tischgebe* (*The Mealtime Prayer*) (1885 AD)

Returning Thanks

Likewise also after the meal they shall reverently and with folded hands say:

O give thanks unto the Lord, for He is good; for His mercy endureth forever. He giveth food to all flesh; He giveth to the beast his food, and to the young ravens which cry. He delighteth not in the strength of the horse; He taketh not pleasure in the legs of a man. The Lord taketh pleasure in them that fear Him, in those that hope in His mercy.

Then the Lord's Prayer and the prayer here following:

We thank Thee, Lord God, Father, through Jesus Christ, our Lord, for all Thy benefits, who livest and reignest forever and ever. Amen.

Jan Steen's *The Prayer Before the Meal* (1660 AD)

TABLE OF DUTIES

*Certain passages of Scripture for various holy orders
and positions, admonishing them about
their duties and responsibilities*

Rafael's *Vermählung Maria* (1504 AD)

Benozzo Gozzoli's *Triumph des Hl. Thomas von Aquin über Averroes*
(1468–1484 AD)

For Bishops, Pastors, and Preachers

A bishop must be blameless, the husband of one wife, vigilant, sober, of good behavior, given to hospitality, apt to teach; not given to wine, no striker, not greedy of filthy lucre; but patient, not a brawler, not covetous; one that ruleth well his own house, having his children in subjection with all gravity; not a novice; holding fast the faithful Word as he hath been taught, that he may be able by sound doctrine both to exhort and to convince the gainsayers. 1 Timothy 3:2 ff; Titus 1:6.

Master of the Virgo inter Virgines' *Saint John the Baptist and a Bishop Saint*
(1480–1495 AD)

What the Hearers Owe to Their Pastors

Even so hath the Lord ordained that they which preach the Gospel
should live of the Gospel. 1 Corinthians 9:14. Let him that is taught
in the Word communicate unto him that teacheth in all good things.
Galatians 6:6. Let the elders that rule well be counted worthy of
double honor, especially they who labor in the Word and doctrine.
For the Scripture saith, Thou shalt not muzzle the ox that treadeth
out the corn; and the laborer is worthy of his reward. 1 Timothy 5:17–
18. Obey them that have the rule over you, and submit yourselves;
for they watch for your souls as they that must give account, that
they may do it with joy and not with grief; for that is unprofitable
for you. Hebrews 13:17.

Lucas Cranach the Elder's *Portrait of Johann the Steadfast* (1509 AD)

Concerning Civil Government

Let every soul be subject unto the higher powers. For the power
which exists anywhere is ordained of God. Whosoever resisteth
the power resisteth the ordinance of God; and they that resist shall
receive to themselves damnation. For he beareth not the sword in
vain; for he is the minister of God, a revenger to execute wrath upon
him that doeth evil. Romans 13:1–4.

Peter Paul Rubens' *The Tribute Money* (Circa 1612 AD)

What Subjects Owe to the Magistrates

Render unto Caesar the things which are Caesar's. Matthew 22:21.
Let every soul be subject unto the higher powers, etc. Wherefore ye
must needs be subject, not only for wrath, but also for conscience'
sake. For, for this cause pay ye tribute also; for they are God's
ministers, attending continually upon this very thing. Render
therefore to all their dues: tribute to whom tribute is due; custom,
to whom custom; fear, to whom fear; honor, to whom honor. Romans
13:1, 5 ff. I exhort, therefore, that, first of all, supplications, prayers,
intercessions, and giving of thanks be made for all men; for kings
and for all that are in authority, that we may lead a quiet and
peaceable life in all godliness and honesty. 1 Timothy 2:1 f. Put
them in mind to be subject to principalities and powers, etc. Titus
3:1. Submit yourselves to every ordinance of man for the Lord's sake,
whether it be to the king as supreme, or unto governors as unto them
that are sent by him, etc. 1 Peter 2:13 f.

Anton Raphael Mengs' *The Dream of St. Joseph* (Circa 1773–1774 AD)

For Husbands

Ye husbands, dwell with your wives according to knowledge, giving honor unto the wife, as unto the weaker vessel, and as being heirs together of the grace of life, that your prayers be not hindered. 1 Peter 3:7. And be not bitter against them. Colossians 3:9.

Giovanni Battista Salvi da Sassoferrato's *The Virgin in Prayer* (1640–1650 AD)

For Wives

Wives, submit yourselves unto your own husbands, as unto the Lord, even as Sarah obeyed Abraham, calling him lord; whose daughters ye are, as long as ye do well, and are not afraid with any amazement. 1 Peter 3:6; Ephesians 5:22.

Claudio Coello's *Holy Family* (Circa 1660–1693 AD)

For Parents

Ye fathers, provoke not your children to wrath, but bring them up in the nurture and admonition of the Lord. Ephesians 6:4.

**Lucas Cranach the Elder's *Adoration of The Child Jesus
by St John the Baptist*** (1530–1540 AD)

For Children

Children, obey your parents in the Lord; for this is right. Honor thy
father and mother; which is the first commandment with promise:
that it may be well with thee, and thou mayest live long on the
earth. Ephesians 6:1–3.

Jacob Willemsz's *Gleichnis von den Arbeitern im Weinberg* (Circa 1660 AD)

For Male and Female Servants, Hired Men, and Laborers

Servants, be obedient to them that are your masters according to the flesh, with fear and trembling, in singleness of your heart, as unto Christ; not with eye-service, as men-pleasers, but as the servants of Christ, doing the will of God from the heart; with good will doing service as to the Lord, and not to men; knowing that whatsoever good thing any man doeth, the same shall he receive of the Lord, whether he be bond or free. Ephesians 6:5 ff; Colossians 3:22.

Caravaggio's *The Incredulity of Saint Thomas* (1601–1602 AD)

For Masters and Mistresses

Ye masters, do the same things unto them, forbearing threatening, knowing that your Master also is in heaven; neither is there respect of persons with Him. Ephesians 6:9; Colossians 4:1.

Guillaume Courtois' *David and Goliath* (1650–1660 AD)

For Young Persons in General

Likewise, ye younger, submit yourselves unto the elder. Yea, all of you be subject one to another, and be clothed with humility; for God resisteth the proud, and giveth grace to the humble. Humble yourselves, therefore, under the mighty hand of God that He may exalt you in due time. 1 Peter 5:5–6.

Ralph Hedley's *The Widow* (1899 AD)

For Widows

She that is a widow indeed, and desolate, trusteth in God, and
continueth in supplications and prayers night and day. But
she that liveth in pleasure is dead while she liveth. 1 Timothy 5:5–6.

Unknown Artist's *Christ and Saint Minas* (Sixth century AD)

For All in Common

Thou shalt love thy neighbor as thyself. Herein are comprehended all the commandments. Romans 13:8 ff. And persevere in prayer for all men. 1 Timothy 2:1–2.

Let each his lesson learn with care,

And all the household well shall fare.

The Litany

from Johann Konrad Wilhelm Löhe

Lord, have mercy upon us.   **Lord, have mercy upon us.**
Christ, have mercy upon us.   **Christ, have mercy upon us.**
Lord, have mercy upon us.   **Lord, have mercy upon us.**
O Christ, hear us.   **O Christ hear us.**
O God, the Father in Heaven,   **Have mercy on us.**
O God the Son, Redeemer of the World;   **Have mercy upon us.**
O God, the Holy Ghost;   **Have mercy upon us.**
Be gracious to us.   **Spare us, good Lord.**
Be gracious to us.   **Help us, good Lord.**

Titian's *Christ and the Good Thief* (Circa 1566)

From all sin
From all error;
From all evil;   **Good Lord, deliver us.**

Peter Paul Rubens' *Christ Triumphant Over Sin and Death*
(Circa 1615–1616 AD)

From the crafts and assaults of the devil;
From sudden and evil death;
From pestilence and famine;
From war and bloodshed;
From sedition and rebellion;
From lighting and tempest;
From all calamity by fire and water;
And from everlasting death: **Good Lord, deliver us.**

Simon Bening's *Temptation of Christ* (Sixteenth century AD)

By the mystery of Thy holy Incarnation;

By Thy Baptism, Fasting, and Temptation;

By Thine Agony and Bloody Sweat;

By Thy Cross and Passion;

By Thy precious Death and Burial;

By Thy glorious Resurrection and Ascension;

And by the coming of the Holy Ghost, the Comforter: **Help us, good Lord.**

Andrea Mantegna's *Christus als Schmerzensmann* (1475 AD)

In all time of our tribulation;
In all time of our prosperity;
In the hour of our death;
And in the day of judgement;   **Help us, good Lord.**
We poor sinners do beseech Thee;   **To hear us, O Lord God.**

Copy of Lucas Cranach the Younger's *Luther on His Deathbed*
(Before 1600 AD)

And to lead and govern Thy holy Christian Church in the right way;

To preserve all pastors and ministers of Thy Church in the true knowledge and understanding of Thy Word, in the holiness of life;

To put an end to all schisms and causes of offense;

To bring into the way of truth all such as have erred, and are deceived;

To beat down Satan under out feet;

To send faithful laborers into Thy harvest;

To accompany Thy Word with Thy Spirit and Grace;

To raise up them that fall, and to strengthen such as do stand;

And comfort and help the weakhearted and the distressed:

We beseech Thee to hear us, good Lord.

(Likely) Fra Angelico's *The Forerunners of Christ with Saints and Martyrs* (Circa 1423-1424 AD)

To give all nations peace and concord;
To preserve our country from discord and contention;
To give to our nation perpetual victory over all its enemies;
To direct and defend our President, and all in authority;
And to bless and keep our magistrates, and all our people:
We beseech Thee to hear us, good Lord.

Domingos Sequeira's *Caesar's Coin* (1790 AD)

To behold and succor all who are in danger, necessity, and tribulation;
To protect all who travel by land or water;
To preserve all women in the perils of childbirth;
To strengthen and keep all sick persons and young children;
To set free all who are innocently imprisoned;
To defend and provide for all fatherless children and widows;
And to have mercy upon all men:

We beseech Thee to hear us, good Lord.

Gustav Spangenberg's *Luther Making Music in the Circle of His Family*
(Circa 1875 AD)

To forgive our enemies, persecutors, and slanderers, and turn their hearts;
To give and preserve to our use the fruits of the earth;
And graciously to hear our prayers:

We beseech Thee to hear us, good Lord.

O Lord Jesus, Son of God;

We beseech Thee to hear us, good Lord.

O Lamb of God, that takest away the sin of the world;

Have mercy upon us.

Wolfgang Kilian's *Die Märtyrer von Nagasaki* (1628 AD)

O Lamb of God, that takest away the sin of the world;
> **Have mercy upon us.**

O Lamb of God, that takest away the sin of the world;
> **Grant us Thy peace.**

Josefa de Óbidos' *The Sacrificial Lamb* (Circa 1670–1684 AD)

O Christ, hear us. **O Christ, hear us.**

Lord, have mercy upon us. **Lord, Have mercy upon us.**

Christ, have mercy upon us. **Christ, have mercy upon us.**

Lord, have mercy upon us. **Lord, have mercy upon us. Amen.**

The Lord's Prayer Shall Follow

Lavinia Fontana's *Christ with the Symbols of the Passion* (1576 AD)

Scriptural Meditation
Using Beauty and Prayer

Jean-Baptiste Marie Pierre's *Nativity* (Later 18th century)

FOR HEALTH FOR ALL PEOPLE ✝ St. John 5:1–9

After this there was a feast of the Jews, and Jesus went up to Jerusalem. Now there is in Jerusalem by the Sheep Gate a pool, in Aramaic called Bethesda, which has five roofed colonnades. In these lay a multitude of invalids—blind, lame, and paralyzed. One man was there who had been an invalid for thirty-eight years. When Jesus saw him lying there and knew that he had already been there a long time, he said to him, "Do you want to be healed?" The sick man answered him, "Sir, I have no one to put me into the pool when the water is stirred up, and while I am going another steps down before me." Jesus said to him, "Get up, take up your bed, and walk." And at once the man was healed, and he took up his bed and walked.

In the name of the Father, and of the ✝ Son, and of the Holy Spirit.

O God, the Creator and Preserver of all, we humbly implore that You make Your ways known to all people and give Your saving health to all nations. Especially, we pray for Your holy catholic church, that it might be governed and guided by Your Holy Spirit, that all who profess the holy Christian faith may be led into the way of truth, and hold the faith in unity of spirit, in the bond of peace, and in righteousness of life; through Jesus Christ, our Lord. *Amen.*

Washington Allston's *Christ Healing the Sick* (1813 AD)

FOR HEALTH CARE PROFESSIONALS ✝ Jeremiah 17:7–9, 13, 14

"Blessed is the man who trusts in the Lord, whose trust is the Lord. He is like a tree planted by water, that sends out its roots by the stream, and does not fear when heat comes, for its leaves remain green, and is not anxious in the year of drought, for it does not cease to bear fruit." The heart is deceitful above all things, and desperately sick; who can understand it?

O Lord, the hope of Israel, all who forsake you shall be put to shame, those who turn away from you shall be written in the earth, for they have forsaken the Lord, the fountain of living water.

Heal me, O Lord, and I shall be healed; save me, and I shall be saved, for you are my praise.

In the name of the Father, and of the ✝ Son, and of the Holy Spirit.

Lord Jesus Christ, Great Physician and Healer of the sick, give skill, wisdom, and gentleness to all physicians, surgeons, nurses, emergency medical technicians, and all those who care for the sick and suffering, that, always bringing Your healing presence with them, they may not only heal, but shine the lamp of hope in the darkest hours of fear and distress. We pray this for Your name's sake. *Amen.*

Heinrich Hofmann's *The Great Physician at Work* (1890 AD)

FOR THE AGED AND SICK ✝ St. Luke 2:25-32

Now there was a man in Jerusalem, whose name was Simeon, and this man was righteous and devout, waiting for the consolation of Israel, and the Holy Spirit was upon him. And it had been revealed to him by the Holy Spirit that he would not see death before he had seen the Lord's Christ. And he came in the Spirit into the temple, and when the parents brought in the child Jesus, to do for him according to the custom of the Law, he took him up in his arms and blessed God and said, "Lord, now you are letting your servant depart in peace, according to your word; for my eyes have seen your salvation that you have prepared in the presence of all peoples, a light for revelation to the Gentiles, and for glory to your people Israel."

In the name of the Father, and of the ✝ *Son, and of the Holy Spirit.*

Almighty God, who looks down in Fatherly love upon all who suffer, we ask You to hear our prayer for those whose increase of years bring them any sickness or pain, and especially for [**Name**], who is in need of Your divine mercy. Grant to [**him/her**] Your help in spirit and in body, and make [**him/her**] to know that Your everlasting arms support [**him/her**]. On all those who love [**him/her**] have compassion, O Lord; give them strength and comfort, and help them in their tribulation to cast all their care upon You who cares for them; through Jesus Christ, our Lord. *Amen.*

José de Ribera's *Saint Simeon with the Christ Child* (1647 AD)

So Jesus again said to them, "Truly, truly, I say to you, I am the door of the sheep. All who came before me are thieves and robbers, but the sheep did not listen to them. I am the door. If anyone enters by me, he will be saved and will go in and out and find pasture. The thief comes only to steal and kill and destroy. I came that they may have life and have it abundantly. I am the good shepherd. The good shepherd lays down his life for the sheep. He who is a hired hand and not a shepherd, who does not own the sheep, sees the wolf coming and leaves the sheep and flees, and the wolf snatches them and scatters them. He flees because he is a hired hand and cares nothing for the sheep. I am the good shepherd. I know my own and my own know me, just as the Father knows me and I know the Father; and I lay down my life for the sheep. And I have other sheep that are not of this fold. I must bring them also, and they will listen to my voice. So there will be one flock, one shepherd. For this reason the Father loves me, because I lay down my life that I may take it up again. No one takes it from me, but I lay it down of my own accord. I have authority to lay it down, and I have authority to take it up again. This charge I have received from my Father."

In the name of the Father, and of the † *Son, and of the Holy Spirit.*

Almighty God, whose blessed Son Jesus Christ went about doing good and healing all manner of sickness and infirmity among the people, continue, we implore You, this gracious work among us, especially among the aged in the hospitals, nursing homes, and hospices of our land. Cheer and heal them, especially [**Name**] for whom we pray, according to Your good will. Grant to all doctors, nurses, and caregivers wisdom and skill, sympathy and patience; and send Your blessing on all who labor to prevent suffering; through Jesus Christ, our Lord. *Amen.*

Beuron Abteikirche Vorhalle's *Tympanongemälde in der Vorhalle:*
Christus als guter Hirte (Date unknown)

FOR THE WORRIED AND THOSE WHO HURT ✝ St. Matthew 6:25-34

[Jesus said,] "Therefore I tell you, do not be anxious about your life, what you will eat or what you will drink, nor about your body, what you will put on. Is not life more than food, and the body more than clothing? Look at the birds of the air: they neither sow nor reap nor gather into barns, and yet your heavenly Father feeds them. Are you not of more value than they? And which of you by being anxious can add a single hour to his span of life? And why are you anxious about clothing? Consider the lilies of the field, how they grow: they neither toil nor spin, yet I tell you, even Solomon in all his glory was not arrayed like one of these. But if God so clothes the grass of the field, which today is alive and tomorrow is thrown into the oven, will he not much more clothe you, O you of little faith? Therefore do not be anxious, saying, 'What shall we eat?' or 'What shall we drink?' or 'What shall we wear?' For the Gentiles seek after all these things, and your heavenly Father knows that you need them all. But seek first the kingdom of God and his righteousness, and all these things will be added to you. Therefore do not be anxious about tomorrow, for tomorrow will be anxious for itself. Sufficient for the day is its own trouble."

In the name of the Father, and of the ✝ Son, and of the Holy Spirit.

O God, we ask Your help for all those who are sad, worried, or perplexed in any way, especially Your servant [**Name**], for whom we pray. Grant to [**him/her**] peace and a firm trust in You, and grant to us a greater understanding and sympathy for the hurts and problems of others. Give us courage to identify ourselves with the troubled and sorrowful of the world; through Jesus Christ, our Lord. *Amen.*

**From *The Art Bible Comprising the Old and New Testaments:
With Numerous Illustrations* (1896 AD)**

FOR THOSE IN NURSING HOMES & CARE FACILITIES ✝ St. John 19:23-27

When the soldiers had crucified Jesus, they took his garments and divided them into four parts, one part for each soldier; also his tunic. But the tunic was seamless, woven in one piece from top to bottom, so they said to one another, "Let us not tear it, but cast lots for it to see whose it shall be." This was to fulfill the Scripture which says,

"They divided my garments among them, and for my clothing they cast lots." So the soldiers did these things, but standing by the cross of Jesus were his mother and his mother's sister, Mary the wife of Clopas, and Mary Magdalene. When Jesus saw his mother and the disciple whom he loved standing nearby, he said to his mother, "Woman, behold, your son!" Then he said to the disciple, "Behold, your mother!" And from that hour the disciple took her to his own home.

In the name of the Father, and of the ✝ Son, and of the Holy Spirit.

Almighty God and Father, whose Son Jesus cared for His mother, even at the cross, look down, we implore You, and, in Your mercy, behold all whose increasing years cause them to dwell in a home where they can receive the care they need, especially [**Name**], Your servant, for whom we pray. May [**he/ she**] continue to be honored and loved as Your dear child, and may those who serve [**him/her**] ever remember that, in ministering to [**him/her**], they minister to You. Help Your servant to have patience and trust in You; through Jesus Christ, our Lord. *Amen.*

James Tissot's *The Sorrowful Mother* (1886–1894 AD)

FOR THOSE IN HOSPICE CARE ✝ St. John 11:1–7

Now a certain man was ill, Lazarus of Bethany, the village of Mary and her sister Martha. It was Mary who anointed the Lord with ointment and wiped his feet with her hair, whose brother Lazarus was ill. So the sisters sent to him, saying, "Lord, he whom you love is ill." But when Jesus heard it he said, "This illness does not lead to death. It is for the glory of God, so that the Son of God may be glorified through it."

Now Jesus loved Martha and her sister and Lazarus. So, when he heard that Lazarus was ill, he stayed two days longer in the place where he was. Then after this he said to the disciples, "Let us go to Judea again."

In the name of the Father, and of the ✝ Son, and of the Holy Spirit.

O Father of all, You promise never to leave us nor forsake us. We pray for Your servant [**Name**], who has been placed into hospice care, and we commend [**him/her**] to Your good and gracious will. Strengthen [**him/her**] with Your steadfast love and mercy, encourage us by [**his/her**] example, and strengthen us by [**his/her**] fellowship, that with [**him/her**] we may be found worthy in Christ to share in life everlasting; through the same Jesus Christ, our Lord, who lives and reigns with You and the Holy Spirit, one God, now and forever. *Amen.*

Alexey Venetsianov's *Communion of Dying* (1839 AD)

FOR THOSE NEAR DEATH ✝ St. Luke 24:2–7

And they found the stone rolled away from the tomb, but when they went in they did not find the body of the Lord Jesus. While they were perplexed about this, behold, two men stood by them in dazzling apparel. And as they were frightened and bowed their faces to the ground, the men said to them, "Why do you seek the living among the dead? He is not here, but has risen. Remember how he told you, while he was still in Galilee, that the Son of Man must be delivered into the hands of sinful men and be crucified and on the third day rise."

In the name of the Father, and of the ✝ Son, and of the Holy Spirit.

Heavenly Father, give to Your servant a blessed death in the faith. Forgive [**his/her**] sins. Strengthen [**him/her**] for this, [**his/her**] last hour. Sustain [**him/her**] in [**his/her**] agony. Give [**him/her**] the confidence of Your promises that never fail. Send Your holy angels to carry the soul of Your servant to Your face, and the perfect joys of heaven. Protect [**his/her**] body to the day of the resurrection of all flesh. Give to us who live the confidence to die in Your name, and depart in peace, knowing that Your Son Jesus is the resurrection and the life. *Amen.*

Antiveduto Gramatica's *Mary Magdalene at the Tomb* (1620–1622 AD)

FOR PATIENCE ✝ Job 2:7-10

So Satan went out from the presence of the Lord and struck Job with loathsome sores from the sole of his foot to the crown of his head. And he took a piece of broken pottery with which to scrape himself while he sat in the ashes. Then his wife said to him, "Do you still hold fast your integrity? Curse God and die." But he said to her, "You speak as one of the foolish women would speak. Shall we receive good from God, and shall we not receive evil?" In all this Job did not sin with his lips.

In the name of the Father, and of the ✝ Son, and of the Holy Spirit.

O Holy Spirit, You promise to bear fruit in the lives of Your people by the gift of baptism. Teach us to wait for You, and give us the confidence that You will not cast us off forever, but that You will hear and answer our prayers, that we may bear the fruit of patience and longsuffering. *Amen.*

Albrecht Dürer's *Job and His Wife* (Circa 1504 AD)

FOR THOSE WHO MOURN ✝ St. John 11:20-27

So when Martha heard that Jesus was coming, she went and met him, but Mary remained seated in the house. Martha said to Jesus, "Lord, if you had been here, my brother would not have died. But even now I know that whatever you ask from God, God will give you." Jesus said to her, "Your brother will rise again." Martha said to him, "I know that he will rise again in the resurrection on the last day." Jesus said to her, "I am the resurrection and the life. Whoever believes in me, though he die, yet shall he live, and everyone who lives and believes in me shall never die. Do you believe this?" She said to him, "Yes, Lord; I believe that you are the Christ, the Son of God, who is coming into the world."

In the name of the Father, and of the ✝ Son, and of the Holy Spirit.

O Lord Jesus Christ, You are raised from the dead and seated at the Father's right hand. Send Your Holy Spirit, the Comforter, to those who mourn. Give them the confidence of Your promises, the promise of the forgiveness of sins, the resurrection of the body, and the life everlasting. Give us faith in Your word and promises, that we might come to the joys of those who have gone through death to Your eternal life, for You live and reign with the Father and the Holy Spirit, one God, now and forever. *Amen.*

Nikolai Ge's *Maria, Sister of Lazarus, Meets Jesus Who is Going to Their House* (1864 AD)

FOR THOSE WHO TRAVEL ✝ Joshua 5:6–7

For the people of Israel walked forty years in the wilderness, until all the nation, the men of war who came out of Egypt, perished, because they did not obey the voice of the Lord; the Lord swore to them that he would not let them see the land that the Lord had sworn to their fathers to give to us, a land flowing with milk and honey. So it was their children, whom he raised up in their place, that Joshua circumcised. For they were uncircumcised, because they had not been circumcised on the way.

In the name of the Father, and of the ✝ Son, and of the Holy Spirit.

Heavenly Father, Your Son Jesus has promised to be with us always, even to the end of the age. Be with us as we travel. Send Your angels to protect and keep us from all dangers. Bless our going out and our coming in, from this time forth, even forevermore. *Amen.*

Peter Paul Rubens' *The Israelites Gathering Manna in the Desert*
(Circa 1626–1627 AD)

FOR WISDOM ✝ St. Matthew 2:7-12

Then Herod summoned the wise men secretly and ascertained from them what time the star had appeared. And he sent them to Bethlehem, saying, "Go and search diligently for the child, and when you have found him, bring me word, that I too may come and worship him." After listening to the king, they went on their way. And behold, the star that they had seen when it rose went before them until it came to rest over the place where the child was. When they saw the star, they rejoiced exceedingly with great joy. And going into the house, they saw the child with Mary his mother, and they fell down and worshiped him. Then, opening their treasures, they offered him gifts, gold and frankincense and myrrh. And being warned in a dream not to return to Herod, they departed to their own country by another way.

In the name of the Father, and of the ✝ Son, and of the Holy Spirit.

O Lord, You have promised that if anyone lacks wisdom, they need only ask, and You will provide. We need wisdom. Give it to us. Teach us to fear You, to love You, to trust in You in all our ways. Make our path straight. Keep our feet from falling. Teach us according to Your word. *Amen.*

Bernardo Cavallino's *Adoration of the Magi* (1630-1656 AD)

FOR HUMILITY ✝ St. Luke 1:46–55

And Mary said, "My soul magnifies the Lord, and my spirit rejoices in God my Savior, for he has looked on the humble estate of his servant. For behold, from now on all generations will call me blessed; for he who is mighty has done great things for me, and holy is his name. And his mercy is for those who fear him from generation to generation. He has shown strength with his arm; he has scattered the proud in the thoughts of their hearts; he has brought down the mighty from their thrones and exalted those of humble estate; he has filled the hungry with good things, and the rich he has sent away empty. He has helped his servant Israel, in remembrance of his mercy, as he spoke to our fathers, to Abraham and to his offspring forever."

In the name of the Father, and of the ✝ Son, and of the Holy Spirit.

Dear Father in heaven, You cast down the proud and lift up the humble. Humble us with Your law. Lift us up with Your gospel. Keep us in Your kindness in life and in death, that knowing Your love, we might begin to love You and our neighbor. *Amen.*

Philippe de Champaigne's *L'Annonciation* (1644 AD)

FOR THE HOLY SPIRIT ✝ Acts 2:1-4

When the day of Pentecost arrived, they were all together in one place. And suddenly there came from heaven a sound like a mighty rushing wind, and it filled the entire house where they were sitting. And divided tongues as of fire appeared to them and rested on each one of them. And they were all filled with the Holy Spirit and began to speak in other tongues as the Spirit gave them utterance.

In the name of the Father, and of the ✝ Son, and of the Holy Spirit.

Dear Jesus, You have promised that the Father will send the Holy Spirit to those who ask. Send us Your Holy Spirit. Cleanse our consciences. Forgive our sins. Grant Your word to abide in us and bear in us the fruit of repentance and faith. Show us our sin. Strengthen our faith in Your promises. Keep us steadfast in Your word. *Amen.*

Jean II Restout's *Pentecost* (1732 AD)

FOR GRACE ✝ Romans 3:21–26

But now the righteousness of God has been manifested apart from the law, although the Law and the Prophets bear witness to it— the righteousness of God through faith in Jesus Christ for all who believe. For there is no distinction: for all have sinned and fall short of the glory of God, and are justified by his grace as a gift, through the redemption that is in Christ Jesus, whom God put forward as a propitiation by his blood, to be received by faith. This was to show God's righteousness, because in his divine forbearance he had passed over former sins. It was to show his righteousness at the present time, so that he might be just and the justifier of the one who has faith in Jesus.

In the name of the Father, and of the ✝ Son, and of the Holy Spirit.

O Lord, whose mercy is new every morning, and whose faithfulness is great, give us grace this day to rejoice in Your kindness and know Your love. Smile upon us, now and always. *Amen.*

Francisco de Zurbarán's *Saint Luke as a Painter before Christ on the Cross*
(1630–1639 AD)

FOR CHILDREN ✝ Exodus 12:12–13

For I will pass through the land of Egypt that night, and I will strike all the firstborn in the land of Egypt, both man and beast; and on all the gods of Egypt I will execute judgments: I am the Lord. The blood shall be a sign for you, on the houses where you are. And when I see the blood, I will pass over you, and no plague will befall you to destroy you, when I strike the land of Egypt.

In the name of the Father, and of the ✝ Son, and of the Holy Spirit.

Almighty God and Father, we thank and praise You for the blessing of every child born to woman. Bless these children, that they might hear Your word and grow in grace. We humbly implore that You send Your angels to guard and keep them from all harm, that they respect and remain obedient to their parents, and that by Your word and Spirit they remain in the one true faith all the days of their lives; through Jesus Christ, our Lord. *Amen.*

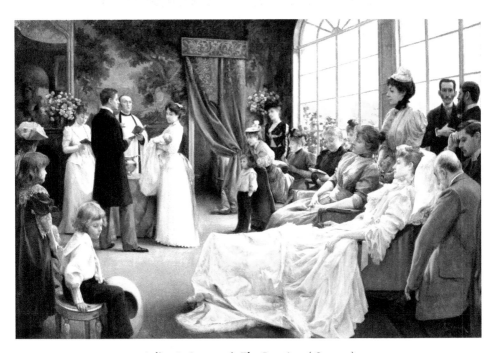

Julius L. Stewart's *The Baptism* (1892 AD)

Gaven Mize is the author of confessional, liturgical, and catechetical books for the family and the church. It is his and his family's desire and passion to produce these books and other materials to aid familial formative growth in the grace and truth of our Lord Jesus Christ. Pastor Mize has authored the children's book *My Little ABC Liturgy Book* for the youngest of our catechumens and looks forward to writing for other age groups.

Pastor Mize has been serving at the altar, font, and pulpit of Augustana Evangelical Lutheran Church in Hickory, North Carolina, since 2014. He married Ashlee at Augustana on October 17, 2015, and they are the parents of Oliver Augustine. Ashlee and Oliver have taught Pastor Mize more about beauty than has any painting made by human hands.

Pastor Mize is also thankful for his parents, Roscoe and Beth Mize, whose love and devotion to their children have opened doors to opportunities neither could have imagined without them.

CPSIA information can be obtained
at www.ICGtesting.com
Printed in the USA
LVOW06s1329290817
546816LV00024B/101/P